Praise for *Breakthrough Marketing Plans*

"A simple, powerful roadmap to creating a simple, powerful marketing plan."
—Professor John Quelch, Senior Associate Dean,
Harvard Business School

"Tim Calkins provides the practical guidance that marketers are longing for. This book lays out a clear path to creating marketing plans that will get supported, and more importantly, drive results."
—Ed Buckley, Vice President, Marketing, UPS

"Stunningly simple. A great guide for anyone who strives to have clarity and impact from their marketing strategies—from the CEO to an entry level marketer. Tim Calkins is an academic with a real world view."
—Randy Gier, Chief Consumer Officer, Dr Pepper Snapple Group

"I highly recommend this book to marketing and brand managers to help them create really pointed and impactful marketing plans."
—Philip Kotler, S.C. Johnson & Son Professor of International Marketing,
Kellogg School of Management

"For new marketers and experienced practitioners, *Breakthrough Marketing Plans*, provides a practical roadmap for developing effective marketing plans that actually serve as daily action guides rather than dusty shelf ornaments."
—M. Carl Johnson III, Senior Vice President and Chief Strategy Officer,
Campbell Soup Company

"Tim Calkins is an award-winning professor and marketer. He knows why most plans fails and what needs to be done to make them useful: set measurable goals, choose a strategy and support it, develop key tactics, and keep it short. *Breakthrough Marketing Plans* is a wonderfully useful book that will change the way marketers and marketing students operate. Read it: it will make you a better marketer!"
—Pierre Chandon, Associate Professor of Marketing, INSEAD

"Tim demystifies and simplifies the critical exercise of driving out world class marketing strategies and executional plans…a must-read for any marketer needing help in articulating a strategy that is about both words and actions, and a must read for any CEO or CMO looking to establish a consistent marketing dialog throughout their organization."
—Scott M. Davis, Senior Partner, Prophet

"Tim Calkins offers an invaluable resource in the time-starved lives of today's marketing professionals."
—Jeffrey Cohen, Global Vice President of Marketing, CIBA VISION

"Tim Calkins has successfully distilled all the marketing theory behind powerful marketing plans into a very pragmatic approach that will not only help guide novice marketers but also will remind experienced marketing leaders of the core fundamentals to driving business growth."
—Paul Groundwater, Vice President, Global Brand Leader, Trane, Inc.

"Practical, action-oriented, to the point. *Breakthrough Marketing Plans* is a valuable tool for marketing professionals and business leaders alike."
—Pete Georgiadis, President & CEO, Synetro Group

BREAKTHROUGH MARKETING PLANS

HOW TO STOP WASTING TIME AND START DRIVING GROWTH

Tim Calkins

Kellogg School of Management

BREAKTHROUGH MARKETING PLANS
Copyright © Tim Calkins, 2008.

First published in 2008 by
PALGRAVE MACMILLAN®
in the US—a division of St. Martin's Press LLC,
175 Fifth Avenue, New York, NY 10010.

Where this book is distributed in the UK, Europe and the rest of the world,
this is by Palgrave Macmillan, a division of Macmillan Publishers Limited,
registered in England, company number 785998, of Houndmills,
Basingstoke, Hampshire RG21 6XS.

Palgrave Macmillan is the global academic imprint of the above companies
and has companies and representatives throughout the world.

Palgrave® and Macmillan® are registered trademarks in the United States,
the United Kingdom, Europe and other countries.

ISBN-13: 978-0-230-60757-6 paperback
ISBN-10: 0-230-60757-8 paperback
ISBN-13: 978-0-230-60756-9 hardcover
ISBN-10: 0-230-60756-X hardcover

Library of Congress Cataloging-in-Publication Data

Calkins, Tim.
    Breakthrough marketing plans : how to stop wasting time and start
driving growth / by Tim Calkins.
        p. cm.
      ISBN 0-230-60756-X—ISBN 0-230-60757-8
      1. Marketing—Planning. I. Title.

HF5415.13.C253 2008
658.8'02—dc22   2008001590

A catalogue record of the book is available from the British Library.

Design by Newgen Imaging Systems (P) Ltd., Chennai, India.

First edition: September 2008

10 9 8

Printed in the United States of America.

For Carol, Claire, Charlie, and Anna

Contents

INTRODUCTION

I have been writing and reviewing marketing plans for more than 15 years, and I have been teaching people how to write good marketing plans for more than a decade. During this time I have reviewed more than 3,000 different marketing plans, from organizations all around the world. That's a lot of marketing plans.

Breakthrough Marketing Plans has evolved from what I have learned during that time. The book is built on three very simple insights.

First, marketing plans are important for every organization and every marketer. Indeed, it is virtually impossible to be a successful marketing leader today if you can't create a clear and effective plan and then gain support for it from senior management and your cross-functional team.

Second, a startling portion of the marketing plans being written today are a complete waste of time. Many should be simply put in the trash or, better yet (from an environmental perspective), the recycle bin. Despite the fact that people and organizations frequently spend months and months working on a marketing plan, the final document often contributes virtually nothing. All too many marketing plans are simply reviewed in a perfunctory way and then quickly put on a shelf, where they function as highly effective dust-gathering devices. This is waste of time and money, and, considering the power of a good marketing plan, a stunning missed opportunity.

Third, creating a good marketing plan is really not all that complicated; the theories behind accomplishing this task reflect a good deal of common sense. Indeed, the very best marketing plans are strikingly simple; they are short, easy to follow, and simple to understand.

I suspect that after reading this book you'll say to yourself, "Well, that seems pretty obvious." And you would be absolutely correct; the basic principles behind creating a good marketing plan are not mind-numbingly complex. However, despite this fact, many marketing plans do not follow the basic principles; far too many plans fall victim to the problems described in this book. As one of my students wrote in a class evaluation form, "The strategies discussed were very intuitive and based on common sense. The fact that I could not come up with any of the strategies on my own further showed that common sense, after all, is not very common."

This book has two goals. The first goal is to highlight the fact that many marketing plans are completely ineffective, and there is an urgent need for change. The second goal is to help people create stronger plans—marketing plans that will be supported and will drive strong results in the market.

WHO NEEDS IT?

This is a book for those who create or review marketing plans. This includes people at large and small organizations, people at for profit and not-for-profit organizations, and people at new companies and old companies. It includes people who work in marketing, of course, but it also includes people from other functions. Indeed, anyone who writes or reviews a marketing plan can benefit from this book.

Breakthrough Marketing Plans is primarily for people new to writing marketing plans, such as business school students and people transitioning into marketing from other functions. For these individuals, this book is an introduction to marketing plans and guide for what to do and what not to do.

This book is also valuable for more seasoned marketers—people who are familiar with marketing plans and the marketing planning process. For these people, *Breakthrough Marketing Plans* has a slightly different purpose: to highlight how marketing plans go awry and help improve them. After reading this book some people will want to completely rethink how they approach marketing plans and adopt these ideas.

Finally, this book is for senior executives, the people accountable for leading an organization and delivering results. Senior managers are, at the end of the day, the people who ultimately approve marketing plans and the people who are most accountable for the results. These are also some of the people who are most frustrated by the plans currently being written. Some senior executives may want to use the ideas in this book to improve the marketing plans being written in their organization. Others may use the book to create a formal marketing planning process if one doesn't already exist.

Importantly, not everyone will agree with the ideas in this book. People wedded to the traditional marketing plan format, for example, may well reject the ideas presented here. this book is a call for change, and many people simply don't like change. But those willing to look at things in a fresh way, read on.

USING THIS BOOK

If you're working on a marketing plan that's due in the near future, flip directly to chapter 8. This chapter provides a template for a marketing plan; if time is short, simply follow the template provided and get to work. You will find the template is a pretty good starting point. It is not as simple as it looks, but the template will get you moving in the right direction.

If you don't know whether you should be worrying about marketing plans in the first place, start with chapter 1. This chapter explains what a marketing plan actually is and why every organization and every product needs one.

If you have a bit more time, you can immerse yourself more fully in the topic and the theories. Chapter 2 explains why so many marketing plans are a waste of time; it describes the typical marketing plan and highlights why it is frequently a fairly stunning miss. Chapter 2 also explores the factors that create weak plans, and it examines this rather important question: Why do smart, experienced people create terrible marketing plans? Chapter 3 reviews the key elements of a marketing plan. Chapter 4 describes the characteristics of the best marketing plans.

Chapter 5 looks at the marketing planning process and presents an eight-step approach. Chapter 6 provides advice and suggestions on writing a good plan, and chapter 7 does the same for presenting a marketing plan.

Chapters 8, 9, 10, and 11 provide tools and answer questions. Chapter 8 presents a marketing plan template. Chapter 9 lays out an example of a good marketing plan. Chapter 10 presents 20 different strategic initiatives to get you thinking about things that you can do to build your business. Chapter 11 reviews frequently asked questions.

* * *

Creating a strong marketing plan is a critical marketing leadership skill, but far too many people do a miserable job at it. The ideas in this book can help marketers create plans that are approved and supported and, most importantly, drive strong results in the market. The ideas may also encourage more than a few people to deposit their current marketing plans in the recycling bin and start over.

CHAPTER 1

Who Needs a Marketing Plan, Anyway?

I don't play golf. I've spent a few hours at a driving range with little success, and I've participated in a game of scramble with colleagues. But I have never seriously played the game, and I don't expect to take it up any time soon. I have nothing against golf; of course, it simply is not a priority for me and I don't have the time right now to spend time on things that are not priorities. Time is short. As a result, there is no reason for me to try to improve my golf swing.

This is broadly true, of course; there is no reason to learn something unless you actually need it or will benefit from it in some other way. There is no need to learn how to drive a car if you don't expect to ever drive. There is no reason to work on a foreign language if you don't expect to speak it.

This line of thinking also applies to marketing plans. The only people who should learn how to create a good marketing plan are people who need marketing plans in the first place. So the first question we must answer is this: Why bother? Why learn about creating a strong marketing plan? Who needs marketing plans, anyway? For that matter, who needs marketing?

JUST A CLINICIAN

In 2003, the American Dental Association launched a program called the Institute for Diversity in Leadership. This program was created to build the leadership capabilities of dentists from traditionally underrepresented groups. During the program, participants created and led public service–oriented projects. As a faculty member for the program, I had the opportunity to listen to the very impressive project updates.

One dentist had led a noble program to provide dental services to homeless veterans in San Francisco. The program provided an exceptionally important and valuable service in a very efficient manner. However, there was one problem; the program needed more dentists to volunteer. Without more dentists, it would be impossible for the program to grow, to reach its full potential, and to have a meaningful impact on the pressing human need.

I asked the project leader a rather simple question: "So what are you doing to attract more dentists? How are you going to market the opportunity? What is your marketing plan?"

This led to a rather awkward silence. The dentist shuffled around a bit and looked this way and that. He then rather sheepishly admitted that he had given no thought to marketing the opportunity. He observed, "I'm no marketer. I'm just a clinician."

He knew, and I knew, that though he is indeed a clinician, he is also a marketer. He markets his dental practice every day, and in this particular case, he needed to market his volunteer opportunity.

Marketing is the process of connecting products, services, and ideas to customer needs. It is essential for every organization; if you can't link your product, service, or idea to a customer need, you will not be successful. People don't buy things for no reason. People spend money, energy, and time on things they need or want. In other words, people buy things that provide a benefit.

For some products this is obvious. People buy toothpaste to prevent cavities, have healthy gums, or whiten their teeth. Companies engage consulting firms to provide insights and recommendations and to ultimately improve results and increase profits. People go to a movie to be entertained. There is always a reason for people to do things; people are always in search of a benefit.

This applies to everything; it's hard to imagine something that isn't affected by marketing to some degree. Consumer products are, of course, dependent on marketing. Restaurants depend on marketing. Retailers, banks, cleaners, and circuses depend on marketing. So do politicians, religious leaders, and environmentalists. They all need people to believe there is a reason to support them; there has to be a benefit.

Each year *Advertising Age* publishes a list of 50 notable marketers called "Fifty sharp ideas and the visionaries who saw them through." The list is always fascinating because the individuals come from all sorts of industries: consumer packaged goods, automotive, health, nonprofit, financial services, and more. The 2007 list, for example, included the usual suspects such as Coca-Cola and Vaseline, as well as other more unexpected brands, including the book *The 4-Hour Workweek*, a new commercial airplane (the Boeing Dreamliner), a computer game (*Guitar Hero* II), and a thong (Hanky Panky) (see exhibit 1.1). The list reflects the wide diversity of organizations who field industry-leading marketing efforts.[1]

We are all marketers. As William Luther wrote in his book *The Marketing Plan*, "The central ideas of marketing are universal, and it makes no difference whether we are marketing furnaces, insurances policies, or margarine."[2]

SETTING THE COURSE

Marketing plans set the course for a business; the marketing plan spells out the goals for the business over a certain period and what precisely should be done to achieve the goals.

Exhibit 1.1   2007 *Advertising Age* Marketing 50

The 4-Hour Workweek	7-Eleven
Activia	Alli
Always	Caribou Coffee bar
Chipotle	Chocolate
Claritin-D	Coke Zero
CPK frozen pizza	Crest Pro-Health
CR-V	Doritos
Dreamliner	Energizer
Facebook	*Halo 3*
Guitar Hero II	Havaianas
Hanky Panky	HP computers
Heineken Premium Light	JCPenney
iPhone	Johnnie Walker Blue
Jenny Craig	Laura's Lean Beef
Keen	Moosejaw
Life Is Good	Ray-Ban
Mucinex	Seventh Generation
SIGG	*Skinny Bitch*
Smart Balance	Soleil
Sparks	Special Dark
SpudWare	Stride
SweetLeaf Stevia	Tresemmé
Umpqua	Vaseline
Webkinz	Wrangler Unlimited
Yahoo Answers	Yelp

More than anything, marketing plans are recommendations; a marketing plan states precisely what steps should be taken to drive the business forward. As Sharon D'Agostino, president of Johnson & Johnson's consumer products division, observed about marketing plans, "This is where we're going and this is how we're getting there."

A marketing plan is the point of connection between data and action. It is the place where an executive takes all the information available and turns it into a plan of action for the business.

In many respects, a marketing plan is the focal point. It is where a marketing leader boils down everything that she or he knows about a business and identifies the most important recommendations. Those recommendations are then broken down into all the various tactics and activities of a business.

Ultimately, marketing adds value when it leads to action, because action leads to results. In most companies, profits matter most; when profit results are good, everything works at the organization; bonuses are generous, stock options can grow dramatically in value, promotions come along more frequently, and people are fundamentally happy. The reverse is also true; when profit results are bad, bonuses are lower, the value of the stock options falls, people are under pressure, and people are grumpy. Having seen both scenarios firsthand, I can say that it is far more enjoyable to work on a business when results are good.

Marketing contributes to an organization when it leads to action, and *only* when it leads to action. Knowing a lot about your consumer is a lovely thing, but all that knowledge will add no value if it isn't put into action. Understanding the insights that motivate consumers is interesting and important, but the only way it will have an impact on the business is if the insights are turned into recommendations.

Exhibit 1.2　Role of Marketing Plans

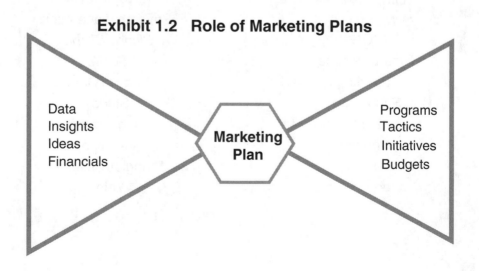

Data
Insights
Ideas
Financials

Marketing Plan

Programs
Tactics
Initiatives
Budgets

Marketing doesn't work unless something actually happens: an advertising campaign goes on television, a new product hits the market, a price changes. One reason the marketing department is sometimes accused of being out of touch with the business is that marketers sometimes focus on insights and never get around to doing anything.

A marketing plan is all about action: what should be done. It is, more than anything, a road map. While writing this book, I spoke with dozens of marketing executives who have reviewed and created marketing plans. The single most common phrase I heard in those interviews was this: a marketing plan is a road map for a business. The words were almost all the same:

> It is a road map for where you are going.
> It's the road map for the future.
> The marketing plan is the road map.
> The reason you do the plan is to lay out the road map.

In any business, it is important to remember that a marketing plan is a road map—it is like a set of directions; it is a description of what needs to be done to get from one place to another: turn left here, turn right here, go 57 miles, turn left, and you are there.

As a result, creating a marketing plan is an opportunity for every business and organization. Marketing is essential for all companies; every organization has to make choices about what to do and what not to do when it comes to reaching customers. As a result, marketing plans are broadly relevant and an opportunity for large companies and small companies, for profit organizations, and for nonprofit organizations.

Marketer Greg Wozniak has seen the broad relevance of marketing plans. He began his career at Kraft Foods, one of the largest food companies in the world. He then moved to Barilla Pasta, a much smaller and privately held company. Later still, he started his own company, selling doors to residential building contractors. At each organization, Greg created and used marketing plans; he had a marketing plan when he was managing hundred million-dollar brands at Kraft, and he had a marketing plan when he was launching his small door company. The plans were different in scope and size, but the basic function was the same: to set the course for the business. As he observed, "Marketing plans are applicable to any business."

ANALYSIS PARALYSIS

Marketing plans are becoming more and more important because the world is getting more and more complicated.

Marketing has never been a simple endeavor. It has never been easy to understand what consumers actually want; people may say one thing but want something else, or they may not be able to envision the future or to even conceive of what is possible. It has never been easy to deal with competition; competitors have been battling it out for market share for centuries. It has never been easy to create powerful communication; this was true in the Middle Ages and it is still true today.

Nonetheless, marketing is getting harder and harder. There are two factors driving this change.

Too Much Data

The first factor making life difficult for marketers is data; there is simply too much information available. Marketers today have access to more data than ever before. For every business, there is a vast amount of information waiting to be used. In some businesses, you can look at sales data by hour, by store, and by product. The amount of information available is stunning, and the amount of time one could spend analyzing this information is infinite. A simple online search on any product yields a vast amount of data. Searching on "Nike" on the Internet results in more than 70 million hits, searching on "Samsung" generates more than 254 million hits, and searching on even a very small brand such as Rolling Rock beer delivers more than 21 million hits.

The issue is only getting worse. The market research industry, for example, is identifying more and more ways to understand customers. A marketer can conduct focus groups, field quantitative studies, complete ethnographies, look at brain scans, do conjoint analyses, and run elaborate multivariant regression analyses. There are new and interesting research techniques appearing all the time, each one creating more and more data and information. With the rise of the Internet and the decrease of computing costs, it is possible to segment consumers into smaller and smaller groups. The concept of true one-to-one marketing is now becoming a possible reality.

The large amount of data available today is a blessing, certainly. Marketers can now make better decisions than ever before; they can dig into information, and they can uncover remarkable insights and then use these insights to create compelling programs. Several years ago, marketers would never have dreamed of having so much information.

However, the vast amount of data is also a curse. If marketers aren't careful, they will simply get lost in the data. They will spend so much time gathering and analyzing the data that they will never get around to drawing conclusions and answering the very basic questions: So what? What does all this mean? What will we do?

When everything can be analyzed, it gets harder and harder to actually come to a conclusion. Analysis is easy. Making a decision is hard. The temptation, of course, is to analyze more and more and to avoid ever reaching a conclusion.

The problem, of course, is that the data doesn't really matter. Having lots of data doesn't necessarily lead to good results on its own. It is just information. What matters is the recommendation: Based on everything we know, what should we *do*?

An Explosion of Choice

The second factor making life difficult is the explosion in choice; marketers now have more options available than ever before.

Making decisions has always been the difficult part of marketing. Ultimately, a marketer has to decide what steps to take to drive sales and build the business. Making these decisions is difficult. Marketing is all about making choices; a company can't do everything. Ultimately, an organization has to decide how to best utilize scarce resources: time, money, attention. This is difficult, because there are hundreds or even thousands of things a marketer could do to sell a product.

The list is only getting longer as technology advances; each day, it seems, another compelling marketing tactic arrives in the market, another wonderful thing to pursue.

Pretend for a moment that you are the brand manager on Heinz ketchup. What are all the things you could do to drive sales and build profits in the United States? The list is long. You could advertise on network television, on one of the four big networks. Alternatively, you could advertise on cable television, on one of dozens of networks. You could advertise in one of the hundreds of magazines on the market, or one of the hundreds of newspapers. You could increase or decrease price or run a promotion. If you are running a promotion, you could run it nationally or just in a particular area, and you could run the promotion continuously for a year or pick just one of the 52 different weeks. You could improve the product so it performs better or reduce the cost of the product. You could change the label or the package. You could create a new flavor. You could launch an entirely new brand or create a subbrand. You could sponsor the Olympics or a local sporting event. You could invest in advertising on the Internet or build a Web site. The list goes on and on and on.

The question isn't which ideas are good ones; many of the ideas would likely work to some degree. Nor is the question which ideas will have immediate impact on the business; many of the ideas would probably do this. Of course, some of the best ideas might not; they may be more focused on the long term. The most important question is this: Which ideas are the best ones to build the business?

Indeed, the only thing that is certain if you are running Heinz ketchup is that you can't pursue all the ideas; trying to do everything will guarantee failure. There isn't enough money to do everything, even on a relatively big brand such as Heinz. More importantly, there isn't enough time in the day; doing more and more things means that each idea gets less and less attention, and it is probably executed less and less well. You have to choose.

Marketing plans help address both of these two challenges. A marketing plan first helps marketers boil down the data to determine what is important. A marketing plan then helps marketers make decisions.

"If you don't know where you're going," the old expression goes, "any road will get you there." This statement is true in life and it is true in marketing; if you don't know what you are trying to accomplish, and what you are trying to do, everything might be a good idea, and it is impossible to decide.

Without a plan, it is very hard to make decisions on programs. Since there is no clear strategy, every program has to be considered on tactical merits; it is impossible to determine what is "on strategy" and what is "off strategy." By default, decisions are then made based on tactics, which is time-consuming and difficult. The result is slow decision making and a lack of synergy across the company, or, as one marketing consultant observed about a client, "It's very haphazard. There is no real logic to how they are going to market."

With a clear marketing plan, however, decisions are easier; a marketer can quickly assess options and rule out those that don't fit the plan. As Unilever marketer Andrew Gross observed, "If the strategy is clear, then you can tell if an idea fits the strategy."

WORKING TOGETHER

One way marketing plans add value is by driving integration across the marketing mix. Integration is fast becoming a "must do" in the world of marketing; different tactics need to work together to maximize the total impact on the business.

This makes obvious sense; tactics should be coordinated and synergistic, so that together the efforts accomplish a mission. The television spots for a brand shouldn't be completely different from the print ads, and the sales brochures shouldn't be completely different from the Web site. Things should work together.

There are two reasons why integration matters. First, integration can increase the impact of a campaign, so the total is greater than the sum of the parts. The theory is that a customer who sees a television ad, and then an online spot, and then a promotion is more likely to grasp the campaign than someone who sees only the promotion, or someone who sees just two television ads.

Second, integration is important to build a strong brand. Brands are the associations linked to a service or product, and the best brands are clearly defined. To create a strong brand, there should be consistent communication so that clear associations are created in the market.

Great television advertising is a good thing, of course, but in the absence of an integrated plan, it will fall short of its potential. A bold pricing move might be a terrific idea, but if it doesn't fit into a broader plan for a business, it will not work; promotion and sales efforts have to support the price move, and the business has to be able to meet changes in demand. A brilliant new product will succeed only if the plan to launch it makes sense.

A wonderful recent example of integration is Toyota; the company leveraged multiple marketing tactics to support the launch of the new Toyota Tundra full-size pick-up truck in 2007. Toyota used television ads on network and cable stations, print ads, online advertising, a Web site, local events, sales brochures, dealer events, and giveaway items to support the launch. All the elements worked together; they communicated the same thing and utilized a consistent creative look. Each tactic was different, but the overall feel was consistent, giving the campaign a far greater impact than if it had been fragmented. All the efforts focused on the same goal: building awareness and trial of the new Tundra among key consumers.

A marketing plan plays a key role in driving integration, because a marketing plan is one place where all the marketing efforts are discussed at the same time. All too often tactics are developed in isolation; the promotion is developed by the promotion agency, the advertising is created by the advertising agency, and the sales meeting is planned and run primarily by the sales team. The risk, then, is that each program will exist in isolation and lose a sense of integration from the customer's perspective.

In a marketing plan, however, the focus is on the total business: What is the overall plan? Once there is a clear plan, it is easier to integrate the tactics, because there is a common understanding of the goals and approach.

It is possible to integrate marketing efforts without a strong marketing plan, but it is much, much harder to do.

All Aboard

At one point in my career I was put in charge of a rather legendary brand, a brand with very high awareness and a long history. The only problem was that the brand had lost its way in the market; sales had slowly and steadily declined for more than a decade. To prop up profits while sales slumped, my predecessors had cut virtually all the marketing spending and put through cost reduction projects that saved money, but at the expense of quality.

Concerned by the long-term trend, I worked with my team to put together a plan to rebuild the business, investing in innovation and marketing, improving product quality, and reaching out to attract a new group of consumers. It was a bold plan, with a very real chance to reverse the long-term business decline.

The problem, of course, was that the plan was costly. The investments were for the future; improving quality and investing in the brand would yield long-term benefits, but it would take time to see the impact in incremental sales. As a result, profits would decline in the short run.

Before moving ahead with the plan, I needed support from senior management in the company to make the short-term investment. Although the plan was exciting, the costs were real and the investments were significant. The challenge for me was clear: lay out the plan in a way that the senior management team would support it.

Without senior management support, the plan couldn't move forward; I could create the plan, but I couldn't pull the trigger.

This is the case in virtually every situation when there is significant money in play; nothing happens without support. Before you make big moves, you need approval from senior management. Any time there are major dollars at stake, senior people want and need to weigh in.

People need support at every level. A marketing assistant can't roll out a new package design without the approval of the brand manager. A category director can't approve a new product launch without the approval of the division manager. A CEO can't move ahead with a dramatic strategic shift without approval from the board of directors and key investors. As Michael Porter, Jay Lorsch, and Nitin Nohria wrote in a recent *Harvard Business Review* article, "A key CEO role is to sell the strategy and shape how analysts and shareholders look at the company. CEOs should not expect that their strategies will be immediately understood or accepted; a constant stream of reiterations, explanations, and reminders will likely be necessary to affect analysts' perceptions."[3]

People also need support from across the organization. Many companies these days are matrix organizations, where people work together with dotted-line relationships. In this type of environment, gaining support for a plan from key functions is essential. An innovation program will fail without the support of the R&D group. An in-store promotion idea will flop if the sales team doesn't agree. A cost-reduction program will not materialize if the operations group doesn't believe it is possible.

Indeed, the only type of organization where you can simply go and do things without approval is a sole proprietorship; in a sole proprietorship you just have to convince yourself that you have a good plan, and this is usually an easy task.

A marketing plan is a key vehicle for gaining support; the marketing plan is the tool managers use to present and gain support for the business. A marketing plan can drive consensus across the organization and serve as a communications vehicle. As marketer Mike Puilcan observed about marketing plans, "The ultimate purpose is to gain agreement."

People need to believe in the plan. A core task of leadership is setting the course, communicating it, and then building support. People need to understand where the business is heading, so that they have confidence in the business and know how their actions contribute to the larger enterprise. General Electric's Jack Welch observed that communicating the direction of a business is a core task of leadership. According to Welch, "People must have the self-confidence to be clear, precise, to be sure that every person in their organization—highest to lowest—understands what the business is trying to achieve."[4] Ford CEO Alan Mulally echoed the point, noting, "I know how successful it can be when a business has a plan, everybody knows the plan, and everybody knows how we are performing against that plan."[5]

This is one of the reasons marketing plans are so important. As Mark Delman, a marketing executive at Adobe, observed, "You need a way to communicate to an organization what you are doing." AspireUp's Roland Jacobs agreed, "A good plan serves as a communications piece."

Is It Worth It?

Creating a marketing plan is a choice. It is not like paying taxes, assembling required financial documents, or paying invoices. An organization can decide to create a marketing plan or not. It is very possible to market a product without a marketing plan. You can simply create a new ad campaign, launch a new product, or roll out a promotion.

So is it worth the time and effort required to actually create and write down a marketing plan? The answer is a resounding yes. Creating a marketing plan will almost certainly produce better results, because the very process of writing a plan forces clarity; it is easy to say, "Oh, we'll do this and that," but it's much harder to write down precisely what needs to happen and why it will work.

More importantly, a marketing plan will drive consensus; it can secure key resources and ensure that all cross-functional team members are aligned. For a leader, this is invaluable.

Spending time creating a plan is an investment that will deliver strong returns.

BE CAREFUL

Writing a very strong marketing plan increases the odds that your plan will be approved. In a sense, this means that you will have the opportunity to try your ideas. As one marketing executive pointed out, "A great plan gives top management confidence in you." Another observed, "You're earning your autonomy with really good plans."

A good plan does not guarantee success; it may improve your odds, but there is no certainty. You have to be somewhat careful. The better you become at creating strong marketing plans, the more likely that you will be given the opportunity to implement the plan. As the old saying goes, "Be careful what you wish for."

A person who is gifted at creating strong plans can take a set of mediocre ideas and get approval. However, although the plan itself might be successful, the bottom-line results are likely to be, well, mediocre.

A good marketing plan gets you to the plate. It gives you the chance to succeed. Moreover, since it is impossible to hit a home run from the dugout, getting to the plate is an essential task. Just don't assume that you'll hit a home run every time you get there.

*　*　*

Every organization in the world needs marketing, and every organization needs a marketing plan. There is so much information in the world and so many tactics that it is almost impossible to make decisions without a plan.

A marketing plan lays out the course for a business, drives integration, and builds support. These are all critical tasks of leadership.

CHAPTER 2

Why So Many Marketing Plans
Are a Waste of Time

"This is an award-winning marketing plan," the executive gushed as he handed me a thick document. I admired its heft, the beautiful cover page, and the perfect binding. I flipped through a few pages; each one was full of information and analysis. "Yes, this one received several prizes in the company," the executive continued. "It is a great piece of work."

I thanked him profusely for letting me review the plan, and after unsuccessfully attempting to squeeze the enormous document into my briefcase, I tucked it under my arm and headed back to my office.

Later that day I sat down and started reading the plan. I read about the industry, the competition, and the challenges facing the business. I read about the distributors and suppliers and all the different trends playing out in the industry. I read about regulatory changes that were on the horizon and potential capacity issues. I read about recent results. In addition, more than anything, I read about consumers: who buys, why they buy, why they don't buy, their motivations and desires.

As I read the plan I quickly realized that the brand faced some very significant business issues; profit was well below goal and even more substantial challenges lay ahead due to tough competitive dynamics. It was a very difficult situation.

Eventually, after many hours, I finally found my way to the second part of the plan, the actual recommendations. This section included a vast array of programs, including promotions, advertising campaigns, sales contests, public relations campaigns, and pricing changes. All of the programs were laid out in minute detail, with the cost calculated down to the dollar. Near the end of the plan there was a complete calendar, showing all the activities planned for the following year.

It took me several days to get through the entire plan, and when I finally finished reading it, I was overwhelmed and exhausted. The plan had gone on for 259 pages, single-spaced. The document contained 45,879 words. It was longer than many novels and about the size of this entire book. It was clearly an impressive document; the product of months of work by a knowledgeable and motivated team.

However, the more I thought about the plan, the more puzzled I became. The first part of the document had identified some major business challenges. The second part presented all sorts of tactics and programs. But there was no link between the two parts; despite the plan's considerable length, there was no explanation of how the recommended tactics would address the issues. Why would the plan work, anyway? How would all the programs deliver improved results?

I phoned the executive who gave me the plan and asked him about the rather distant connection between the first part of the plan, the issues and analysis, and the second part of the plan, the tactics. "Well, you know, that's a pretty good question," he conceded. He thought for a while, and then observed, "Of course, you're probably the first person who has actually read the entire plan."

He was right, of course. The marketing plan, the product of hours and hours of work, had never been read by anyone. Of course, this shouldn't have come as a surprise. How many business executives have time to sit down and read a 259-page, single-spaced document? Most executives run from meeting to meeting, checking e-mail as they go. They hardly have time to flip through the *Wall Street Journal*. So when, precisely, would anyone read a novel-length marketing plan? The thoroughly researched, elegantly produced, and intensely reviewed plan had never been read. Incredibly, the plan—and all the work that went into it—was largely a waste of time.

Sadly, my research and experience suggest this isn't unusual. Although many companies devote an extraordinary amount of time and effort to marketing plans, more often than not, the result is a long, complicated document that says little and is frequently not even read. As Chicago advertising executive Stuart Baum noted, "In many companies, if you put a five-dollar bill between page 16 and page 17 of the marketing plan, no one would ever find it."

The overall situation is rather grim; executives across industries are frustrated with long, tedious, and pointless marketing plans. At best these irrelevant tomes simply consume and waste time and resources. At worst, they suck energy and creativity from an organization.

The discontent spans companies and industries. "Five percent of marketing plans are good," observed Michael McGrath, a marketing executive at pharmaceutical giant Eli Lilly. "Most of them suck wind." Karen David-Chilowicz, a marketing veteran with experience at Prudential and Western Union, is just a tad bit more positive: "Maybe 20 percent of companies do it right. Many have absolutely no clue." Consumer goods marketer and private equity investor Andy Whitman is more direct, declaring simply, "Most of them suck."

This is an enormous problem. For many executives, creating a marketing plan is a time-consuming and frustrating experience, notable mainly for what the process doesn't produce: a clear direction for how a business will build sales and profits. The sad truth is that perhaps most marketing plans are a vast waste of time and money, a long, unwieldy recitation of facts and details. The marketing plan ends up on a bookshelf, unread.

In many companies, marketing is coming under attack; people are raising tough questions about what marketing actually contributes. One sign of the discontent is the growing course of people demanding concrete return on investment figures (ROI) on marketing programs. Another sign is the pace of turnover in the ranks of chief marketing officers (CMOs); a recent study done by executive recruiter Spencer Stuart found that the average tenure for a CMO was just 23.6 months, less than half the average tenure for a CEO.[1]

The typical marketing plan does little to dispel the belief that marketing contributes little to the organization. A marketing plan that is a largely irrelevant collection of facts and data contributes mightily to the view that marketing is largely irrelevant, too. This is a shame, an embarrassment, and an enormous problem for the entire marketing industry.

THE USUAL DOG AND PONY SHOW

If you've worked in marketing for any length of time, you're most likely very familiar with the typical marketing plan; you know the usual show all too well.

The typical marketing plan is a long document, perhaps 100 or 200 pages long, or even more. It is polished. It is usually a PowerPoint presentation. The pages are colorful, full of graphs and charts. The binding—and it is always bound in some fashion—is perfect. The document is labeled with something authoritative, perhaps: "Electronics Division 2009–2010 Marketing Plan." It is clear that the team spent hours and hours creating the document.

The plan starts with the table of contents, which is itself long and detailed, listing the dozens of chapters and sections. The table of contents may go on for two or three pages.

The first section is the situation analysis, and this part makes up the bulk of the plan. The situation analysis reviews virtually all the information the team knows about the business and the category. The depth and breadth of information is astounding, including a review of the product line, an analysis of key competitors, a review of trends in the industry, a discussion of product cost issues, and a recap of recent activities and results. In more customer-focused companies, there is a vast amount of information on customers, ranging from segmentation study results to findings from the latest round of focus groups.

After the situation analysis, the plan moves on to recommendations. These are usually organized around the 4 Ps (price, promotion, place, and product) or around functions (advertising, promotions, sales, and R&D), or both. Often, each one of the sections is written by a different functional group, so the sales group writes the sales section, the operations group writes the operations section, and the new products team writes the new products section.

The recommendations are lengthy; the plan includes all the planned programs for the upcoming year or two. In many cases the tactical detail is extensive. In the advertising section, for example, there may be a five-page discussion of the media plan alone, including several potential media schedules that show possible media-mix combinations. In one version, the media spending is concentrated on network television. In another version, there is a mix of network television, cable television, and radio. In another version, network television is reduced, with Internet advertising expanded.

The plan then moves on to a financial section, where the budget and financial projections are laid out in detail for the next several years. The financial section may include an analysis of cash flow and capital expenditures, and it might show margin trends across multiple dimensions.

The typical plan often comes with an exceptionally robust appendix, which includes all the findings and analysis that didn't make it into the situation analysis or the rest of the plan. Indeed, in some cases there is a page ready to address every possible question someone might ever ask about the business. In one notable example, a team wrote a 100-page marketing plan and then created a 200-page appendix.

After months of development, the marketing team presents this document to senior management. The team reserves the largest available conference room and rehearses extensively in the days leading up to the presentation. The day before the "dog and pony show" is a scramble, as people try to finish the presentation and then run copies. Just making all the needed copies takes much of the day.

On the day of the meeting, the team arrives early to set up the room; they carefully arrange the chairs and tables, make sure breakfast is ready, and double-check that all the props are on hand. As the start time approaches, the marketing team settles in and then the senior executive team arrives. An often substantial number of other interested but tangentially involved people file in, too: the lawyers, the human resources team, and the procurement group. Finally, the lights dim and the team launches into the well-polished show. Sixty people, sometimes more, look on with excitement and anticipation. It is a glorious show to which everyone who's anyone wishes to be invited.

Over the course of the next several hours, the excited and nervous marketing team presents the plan, going through the lengthy presentation page by page. The presenters review the agenda, the situation analysis, and the recommended programs. Various team members stand up to present a few pages, then sit down. The team methodically moves through the slides. Questions, if there are any, are handled smoothly, perhaps with the use of a page from the appendix.

About three hours later, the team wraps up things up, right on schedule. The audience smiles and applauds the team's tremendous work and great ideas. The comments are frequently the same: "This is an impressive plan, and it clearly reflects a tremendous amount of work. Well done!" Or, "It is wonderful to see this kind of analytic and creative thinking on the business.

The team deserves a lot of credit for doing such a good job!" Or, "I am truly impressed with the plan. It won't be an easy year, but I think this plan is a tremendous document." After one or two rather perfunctory questions, everyone then heads off. The marketing team goes out to lunch and takes the afternoon off. And with that, another year's marketing plan passes into history.

A Waste of Time

The problem, of course, is that the entire exercise was largely a waste of time; the business team invested weeks creating the plan, but the plan contributed almost nothing.

The plan failed to set a clear course for the business. Although the team presented lots of data and many insights, there was no theme, and no overall story people could remember. The overall takeaway was, "Wow, you know a lot and are doing a lot of things." This is neither memorable nor distinctive. It is work for the sake of showing the company you are working.

Most important, the plan failed in its most basic task: It didn't gain agreement on the overall direction for the business. The senior executives who reviewed the plan didn't say anything bad about it, but they didn't necessarily endorse it, either. It wasn't actually given the green light.

This lack of support is a huge problem for the people charged with running the business. Without agreement on the plan, each tactical decision comes up for review, discussion, and scrutiny.

This leads to frustration and unproductive discussions when it comes to execution. When presenting a new public relations campaign, for example, a team might hear something like this from a senior executive, "So tell me again, what are the goals for this program? How much are we spending? Do we really need to do this?" The questioning of the tactic reflects a lack of understanding of the broader picture. It is also incredibly frustrating for the team managing the project; it sends them right back to square one.

The lack of agreement also leads to problems when it comes to finalizing financial plans. In many cases, to make the financial targets, spending on marketing programs gets reduced, and generally without a concurrent reduction in sales targets. Of course, when a marketing plan is just a collection of tactics, it seems easy and painless to reduce spending; "Oh, we can run fewer ads or spend less on the Web site."

Therefore, despite the fact that the team invested weeks in a marketing plan, it contributed little. The ornate marketing plan, assembled and bound with such care, was largely a waste of time and effort.

What Went Wrong?

Anytime a commercial airplane crashes, there is an investigation into what happened. The emergency responders locate the black box that recorded everything that occurred leading up the crash, and a team of aviation experts sits down to reconstruct the scene and figure out precisely what happened. More important, perhaps, the experts try to figure out what can be done to prevent future crashes.

The same process can be applied to marketing plans. Why, precisely, do so many marketing plans end up contributing so little? When plans go awry, what happened? What can be done to prevent future incidents?

During the process of researching this book, I asked dozens of marketing and business executives about marketing plans. In particular, I asked them where plans fall short. When a plan doesn't work, what happened? What caused the problem?

From my research, I learned that there are five very common problems or pitfalls. These problems are consistent across industries.

The Top 5 Problems

1. Data, Data, Data
2. Anyone See a Strategy?
3. And *Why* Would We Do That?
4. The Moon Might Be Made of Cheese
5. The CFO Did It

These five problems are almost universal. If you find a weak marketing plan, very often one of the five problems lurks behind the picture. Let's look at these problems in detail.

Data, Data, Data

The biggest problem in many marketing plans is very simple: the plan includes too much data. All too many marketing plans are simply too long and filled with too much information. The plan goes on, and on, and on.

Many marketing plans are 80, 100, or even 200 pages long. The plans contain an extraordinary collection of information, virtually everything that is known about the business. Frequently, the marketing plan itself ends up being stuffed with data, and then it is paired with an even longer appendix.

The situation can quickly become absurd. Marketer Kevin McGahren-Clemens spent more than a decade at Kraft Foods before moving to a smaller food company. He recalled the moment when he realized the marketing plan process was out of control:

> I was on Philadelphia Cream Cheese, and we were going to present the plan. The deck was about 120 or 130 pages, and there were huge filing boxes full of backups. There must have been 1,000 pages. I thought afterwards, Look at all the manpower and stress.

One well-known consumer products company embarked on a marketing plan simplification project, with the focus on getting to very tight, focused plans. The result of the project was that the average marketing plan at the company dropped to 70 pages. This was considered a major step forward. Of course, the plan was still far too long: Who has time to read 70 pages?

Things are really grim when a marketing executive can make this statement with some pride: "We're seeing shorter plans. Some are even down to 90 pages."

The problem is that all the information hurts rather than helps the plan. Too much information creates several problems. First, the data obscures the more important parts of the plan, the actual recommendations. When a set of recommendations is preceded by 80 pages of information and analysis, the recommendations will get lost. Many people will never get to the recommendation at all. Those who do will be exhausted and overwhelmed by the data and complexity.

Second, it takes a lot of time to create a data-intensive plan. As a result, there is a risk that more time will be spent on laying out the data than generating or supporting the actual recommendations. As one executive explained, "So much time is spent trying to gather relevant information that the marketer runs out of time to analyze it and determine the implications for the plan." The result is unfortunate: "There is too much data and too little analysis and implication."

Many people argue that it is better to include more information than less; if nothing else, a large document suggests that the team has been diligent and worked hard. This line of thinking is flawed; added unnecessary information clutters the plans and obscures the recommendation. If the information is not directly relevant to the matter at hand, it should not be in the plan. Mark Shapiro, the CEO of Gladson Interactive and a former general manager at Quaker Oats, lamented, "So many presentations are simply one chart after another."

There are two places where marketing plans can become bogged down with too much information. The first is the situation analysis; this part of the marketing plan all too often goes on and on with no real point. In an effort to do a rigorous situation analysis, the team includes all sorts of information: a list of products, a review of pricing, a deep competitive analysis, an update on new products. Most of it is not needed. Many times, the situation analysis seems like a code for, "Here is all the data we have on this business." As one executive observed, "The temptation is to include every morsel of information gleaned in the market assessment to the detriment of the plan."

The problem today is that there is simply far too much information available on any particular business. Just laying out the basics of a business, the important trends, the competitive situation, and the recent performance can take 80 or 90 pages. However, in reality, these 80 or 90 pages accomplish virtually nothing; the information does not lead directly to a recommendation. One plan I reviewed featured a page with a picture of the brand's four products, ignoring the fact that anyone reviewing the plan would almost certainly already know the existing products. Another plan featured a map of the United States showing the breakout of sales by region. Was the regional sales information particularly important? No. It was simply an attractive and totally irrelevant chart. Most marketing plans would improve substantially if the situation analysis was simply dropped and the plan began with the recommendations.

The second place where plans can bog down is in the tactics. Many marketing plans include very detailed tactical information. The plan includes information on each promotional event, each sales contest, and each public relations initiative. This is all unnecessary.

A good marketing plan should focus on the key initiatives, not the detailed tactics. Indeed, until there is an agreement on the big initiatives there is no point working through all the tactical details. Finalizing the creative for a coupon supporting a new product, for example, doesn't make any sense until it is certain the new product will be launching and supported by the coupon.

If you present detailed tactics, the focus of the discussion can quickly move from the big strategic questions to small tactical questions. This doesn't help anyone. As one marketing executive observed, if you present too many tactics, "suddenly your presentation to management is all about whether the FSI is 25 cents or 50 cents."

The tactical details should be worked out by the business team. The tactical details should not be presented to or reviewed by senior executives. As Roland Jacobs observed, "Senior management is looking to get results. They don't care about a coupon plan." Reviewing detailed program information with senior management is dysfunctional; it suggests the team isn't confident in its ability to execute, and it encourages senior people to get involved in little issues.

The only reason a senior executive needs to review a small tactical decision is if he doesn't trust the team running the business, and this is symptomatic of a much bigger problem.

Anyone See a Strategy?

It is impossible to create a great marketing plan with weak strategic thinking. The strategies are the heart of the plan, the framework around which the entire plan is built. Weak, vague strategies fail to provide any direction, and this will leave a plan adrift.

All too many marketing plans encounter one of three problems when it comes to strategy. The first problem is a complete lack of strategies. The plan jumps directly from the situation analysis to tactics or from objectives to tactics and entirely skips the strategies. This is a problem because the strategies provide the glue that holds the plan together, and without the glue the plan will fall apart. The plan might present an advertising tactic, for example, before there is agreement about why advertising is in the plan at all, or how the advertising fits into the broader picture.

A marketing plan I recently reviewed from one of the world's largest auto companies provided a perfect example of this problem. The plan started with a review of the situation, including an analysis of the competition and trends in the market. It then jumped directly to the tactics: pricing strategy, promotion strategy, and dealer strategy. Missing, of course, was the heart of the plan: the key strategies the team recommended to ensure success.

The second problem is vague or imprecise strategies; strategies that say basically nothing. The strategy is so broad and general that it is meaningless. One plan I read recently, for example, listed one of the strategies as "pricing." This is an empty strategy; it doesn't provide any direction for the business. What about pricing? Another strategy in the same plan was "innovation." What about innovation? The strategy says nothing.

The third problem is having too many strategies. Some plans include 8, 9, or even 11 strategies. This is simply too many. One plan I read featured 17 strategies. The problem here is that an organization cannot focus on 17 things, or even 9 things at once.

Developing strategy is the process of focusing; strategic decision making is all about making decisions. In many ways, an organization that has 15 strategies has none; there is no prioritization, no decision making. A list of 15 strategies is not actually a list of strategies; it is just a list of things.

Conagra's Sergio Pereira noted that having too many strategies is a common problem in marketing plans. He observed, "People always bite off more than they can chew." Adobe's Mark Delman agreed, "It's often 5 objectives and 25 strategies," he says. "The organization just can't handle that."

The problem, however, is that the strategies are the most important part of the plan; this is where managers and senior executives should be placing the majority of their focus.

And Why Would We Do That?

A good marketing plan needs to be persuasive. Someone reading a good marketing plan will understand what the plan is and why it will work. In many plans, however, there is little support for the recommendation. The plan explains *what*, but it doesn't explain *why*.

Since one of the most important reasons to create a marketing plan is to gain support across the organization, a marketing plan needs to have lots of rationale.

One 50-page marketing plan I reviewed recently had 20 pages of recommendations. The plan completely lacked, however, any support for the recommendations.

Marketing is really about selling; a marketer spends his or her time looking for ways to sell a product, service, or idea. Therefore, it is somewhat surprising how often marketers neglect to sell the marketing plan.

Of course, the structure of many marketing plans makes it hard to provide the needed support. For example, the traditional plan, featuring a thorough situation analysis followed by a series of recommendations, leaves little room for rationale; all the data was presented before any recommendations. Connecting the data to the recommendations is left to the reader. This is not the ideal approach.

A good marketing plan provides clear, unambiguous data supporting the recommendations. If the plan is recommending an increase in advertising, the rationale for the spending increase is clear. If the plan is recommending a public relations effort, the thinking behind the recommendation is apparent.

The Moon Might Be Made of Cheese

Many marketing plans fail because they are based on wishful thinking. The plan is so optimistic that it is not credible at all.

Wishful thinking can pop up throughout a plan, from the impact of new products to the power of different marketing ideas to the receptivity of distribution partners to a new program.

Optimism is one of the great downfalls of many business executives, and marketers are perhaps more susceptible than most to its siren call. It is easy and pleasant to simply assume that things will play out as desired; the new product will succeed, competitors will retreat, and customers will eagerly welcome a price increase. However, ignoring the reality of a situation is a certain recipe for trouble. New products generally fail, competitors will almost always complicate your life, and customers will push back against a price increase. Great plans anticipate and incorporate the reality of the situation.

A marketing plan based on optimistic assumptions causes all sorts of problems. First, the plan is rarely credible, so it doesn't get support. Second, the plan rarely works; it doesn't deliver the planned results because things never turn out perfectly. Third, the plan isn't optimal; a more realistic view of the situation would have led to more realistic strategies.

A good marketing plan is based on a realistic view of the situation, the competition, and the capabilities of the company. Assuming that everything will work out fine is both delusional and destructive. As one seasoned marketer observed, "You need to look reality in the eye."

Steven Cunliffe, president of Nestlé's Frozen Foods Division, observed that a weak plan is "... usually disconnected from reality," noting that many plans are full of wishful thinking and lack any substantive analysis of competition.

And he's right. A marketing plan must be grounded in the situation as it exists today, not as someone might wish it would be.

The CFO Did It

The final problem that many marketing plans encounter is too much financial information; the marketing plan becomes essentially a large budgeting document; it is a just a financial planning tool.

Companies need to develop financial forecasts to anticipate and plan for the business. For example, to understand capital needs, a business needs a detailed set of financial projects. In addition, to set reasonable objectives a company needs a thorough set of projects. Budgeting, after all, is a core business task. In most companies, budgets are exceptionally detailed and rigorous, as they should be.

However, detailed financial forecasts are not marketing plans, and they should not travel together. A marketing plan needs to touch on the financials, certainly, but a marketing plan isn't a budget.

Loading too much financial information into a marketing plan creates a simple problem: the numbers overwhelm the strategy. This is a particular problem if your audience is financially inclined. If you present a marketing plan that includes detailed financials to a financially oriented executive, there is a very real chance that the entire conversation will focus on the numbers. Instead of thinking about how precisely a business will compete and what it should focus on, the discussion becomes geared to the financial questions, such as margin trends and cost forecasts.

Reviewing numbers is not the reason to create a marketing plan; detailed financial projections should be the result of a marketing plan, not the input. For example, an advertising budget should be set only when the broader strategy is clear; if there isn't a strategic need for advertising, then there shouldn't be any spending on it regardless of last year's effort.

One executive I spoke to recalled how his division would create thorough and thoughtful marketing plans for each of the key products during the annual planning process. The presentation to the CEO, however, included both marketing plans and the financial budget. As a result, the entire meeting focused on the numbers; the marketing plans were never discussed.

It is tempting to load up a marketing plan with financial information. Financials are factual and easy to obtain. They are also concrete and tangible, as opposed to marketing initiatives and tactics that are often ambiguous and hard to precisely define. It is much easier to present numbers than concepts. Presenting financial forecasts, however, is not the purpose of a marketing plan.

As one expert on marketing plans wrote, "Preoccupation with preparing a detailed one-year plan first is typical of those many companies who confuse sales forecasting and budgeting with strategic marketing planning—in our experience the most common mistake of all."[2]

There needs to be a link between the financials and the marketing plan, of course, but the marketing plan shouldn't be a financial plan.

WHY GOOD PEOPLE CREATE
BAD PLANS

Most people who succeed in marketing are smart, strategic thinkers. Marketing is difficult; understanding consumers and figuring out how to meet their needs while differentiating from competition and driving profits is a major challenge. Therefore, the people who succeed in marketing are generally shrewd business leaders.

Why, then, do smart people create marketing plans that contribute so little? Why do good people create bad plans?

The Easy Road

The first reason why good people create bad plans is simple: it is easy. It isn't hard to create the traditional long, detailed marketing plan. It takes time and effort, of course, but the process is clear: assemble a long, detailed situation analysis, create highly detailed tactical plans with lots of ideas, and produce a glossy, nicely bound document. Indeed, with time, energy, and a good printer, anyone can produce the typical marketing plan, and one that looks polished and thorough to boot.

It is much harder to create a tight, focused marketing plan. Figuring out the key strategies for a business and explaining why they will create positive results is hard work, requiring thought and analysis. A tight marketing plan requires choice and decisiveness, and making choices is hard work. As Procter & Gamble CEO A.G. Lafley observed, "Most human beings and most companies don't like to make choices. And they particularly don't like to make a few choices that they really have to live with. They argue, 'It's much better to have lots of options, right?' "[3]

There Is Safety in Numbers

A long, detailed marketing plan gives a feeling of safety. Many managers take comfort in data; with enough data, they can answer any question. A big deck looks impressive. There is something immensely satisfying about handing out a large presentation; the thunk on the table communicates thoroughness, hard work, and credibility.

I spoke with one marketing executive from Coca-Cola who always strived to have the longest marketing plan in the company. She observed, "You were proud about that."

Showing up with a small, focused marketing plan, by contrast, can be terrifying, because the ideas are clear and apparent. Everything looks simple.

General Electric's Jack Welch appreciates the challenge. "You can't believe how hard it is for people to be simple—how much they fear being simple," he says. "They worry that if they're simple, people will think they are simple-minded. In reality, of course, it's just the reverse. Clear, tough-minded people are the most simple."[4]

Tradition

Every organization has ways of operating. Organizational culture runs deep, especially in organizations that promote from within. As a result, many processes become deeply entrenched in an organization, and marketing planning is one of them.

In many companies, the marketing plan process is a central part of the annual calendar; it has been done for years, and everyone knows what to expect. People plan their vacations around the process.

In this type of environment, there is a huge incentive to simply follow the norms and stick with tradition. Doing something different is risky and scary. Showing up with a 20-page plan when everyone in the company knows that a marketing plan should be 150 pages is scary and dangerous. It is safer and easier to stick with the tradition.

By the Book

Sadly, the existing guides to writing great plans do not help the situation. Most of them actually make it much worse.

Consider, for a moment, one of the leading guides to writing marketing plans, now in its fifth edition. The book is a remarkable 630 pages. The recommended table of contents for a plan goes on for three pages. The guide suggests starting the marketing plan with a marketing audit, and the description of this audit goes on for 154 pages.

Another guide to marketing plans starts off with this dynamic sentence: "The purpose of this book is to assist you in developing a sound and profitable marketing plan by creating a desirable positioning or personality for your business based on your Fact Book, which is an analysis of market economics, competition, customers, and your own business, and then make that personality come alive with the execution of unique-to-your-industry marketing tools."[5] Enough said.

In yet another guide to marketing plans, the author issues a warning: "It is strongly advised, however, that you consult your accountant when considering this section, as the methodology described is quite complex...."[6]

Sadly, these misguided recommendations are not unusual. Managers who look for ways to improve marketing planning find little to fall back on. It is not a surprise that people looking for help writing great marketing plans find little appropriate guidance. In the end they waste vast amounts of time on plans that will have little impact.

Of course, many of the existing guides to writing marketing plans were created by academics, people who have a deep knowledge of business theory and a great appreciation for knowledge and learning. It isn't surprising that their recommendations call for, yes, a focus on knowledge and learning. Missing, however, are the questions facing practicing executives: So what are we going to do? Why will it work, anyway?

* * *

In one of the first commercials ever aired for the Dyson vacuum cleaner, inventor James Dyson explained how most vacuum cleaners suffered from a basic problem. "Ever since the vacuum cleaner was invented, it has had a basic design flaw. Bags, filters, they all clog with dust and then lose suction. The technology simply doesn't work."

The typical marketing plan also suffers from a basic design flaw: it focuses on the details and not on the big picture. It gets lost in the data and the tactics. As a result, the plan ends up being a vast waste of time. It is a wonderful dog and pony show, but it contributes nothing to the business.

CHAPTER 3

What Really Matters: The One-Page Summary

Marketing plans are not all that complicated. A marketing plan is not a book; the goal isn't to create a literary masterpiece that will take its place beside *War and Peace* in the Library of Congress. A marketing plan is a working document, created for a specific purpose: to set the course for a business and to ensure that everyone is on the same page. As marketer Greg Wozniak observed, "It is almost scary how basic it is."

This chapter explains the three key components of a great marketing plan and reviews how the elements can be summarized on one simple page—yes, one page.

GOST: Goals and Objectives, Strategic Initiatives, and Tactics

For people accustomed to creating marketing plans that go on for 200 pages, it is probably an astonishing thought, but a breakthrough marketing plan can be summarized on one page—a page that simply shows the goals and objectives, the strategic initiatives, and the key tactics. This summary can be created by using what I call the GOST framework (Goals and Objectives, Strategic Initiatives, and Tactics). The GOST framework begins with the one or two plan objectives. The objectives then point to the strategic initiatives. And then each strategic initiative points to the tactics supporting that particular initiative.

The GOST framework is a powerful tool and should be part of every marketing plan. The framework does three things particularly well.

First, the GOST framework forces a manager to focus. There isn't room for 8 strategies and 27 tactics. There is room for only one or two objectives, three or four strategies, and two or three tactics for each strategy. This means a manager must go through the process of selecting the most important things. Indeed, if the GOST framework ends up being incredibly complicated, with many strategies and tactics, then the plan isn't focused enough.

Exhibit 3.1   GOST Framework

Goals/Objectives   **Strategic Initiatives**   **Tactics**

Primary objective

Secondary objective

Strategic Initiative 1   —Tactic
—Tactic

Strategic Initiative 2   —Tactic
—Tactic
—Tactic

Strategic Initiative 3   —Tactic
—Tactic

Second, the GOST framework provides an easy way to check that the plan holds together and is internally consistent. By seeing all the key elements on one page, it is easy to test whether the plan is linked and if it will hold together. Obvious problems surface quickly. For example, if there is a strategic initiative with no tactics, it is almost certain that nothing will happen against that initiative. If there are tactics that don't fall under any strategic initiative, the plan may not be focused or complete. If there are many initiatives, the plan is not yet tight.

Third, the GOST framework is a wonderful plan summary. This chart, placed at the beginning and the end of a marketing plan, will summarize all the activities held within the plan itself. This makes it a powerful communication device.

It is important to note, however, that the GOST framework is not a complete plan; it is simply the summary. The GOST framework doesn't include rationale supporting the plan, and it doesn't address financial issues. As a result, just completing the GOST framework is not sufficient; you need the rest of the plan wrapped around it.

But every marketing plan must be laser-focused on the three elements of GOST. The challenge is to cut through all the data, all the information, and all the complexity to directly lay out the core elements.

One marketing executive summed it up by stating that a marketing plan should focus on three simple questions: "What do you want to get done? How are you going to do it? What exactly are you going to do?" Once you answer these questions, then you let the GOST framework do the rest. The following sections help you understand what should be included in each of the three GOST elements.

The Big Picture: Goals and Objectives

A marketing plan should be built around goals and objectives; you can't develop a plan until you know what you're trying to achieve. There is no reason to write a marketing plan if you don't have an objective. A marketing plan is an action-oriented document; the only reason to create a plan is to achieve something. As a result, marketing plans should always start with objectives. Indeed, without an objective the entire planning process is basically just a waste of time.

Goals and objectives are not complicated; the words are interchangeable. The goal or objective is what the plan is trying to achieve. A goal is not a value, principle, or theory. The goal is the desired end result.

A marketing plan should be built around just one or two objectives. A business that has a dozen goals has no focus and no sense of direction. Prioritization isn't clear, and defining success becomes difficult.

A good objective is quantifiable; it is specific and measurable. Good objectives follow the acronym SMART: they are specific, measurable, aggressive, realistic, and time-specific. A good objective has to be specific, which simply means that it must be clear. Vague objectives are not helpful. Measurement is essential; an objective should be easy to measure. Indeed, this is the only way to evaluate success and to measure progress. Good objectives strike a balance between being aggressive and realistic. Moreover, an objective should be time-specific; it should be clear *when* the objective should be achieved. Without a time element, objectives have no urgency. It is a bit like committing to lose weight without committing to a target date; you can always push the target out into the future and have another doughnut or two today.

Show Them the Money

Marketing plans should be built around profit objectives; the plan should focus on the money.

The core challenge for anyone running a business is building profits. Profits ultimately drive a public company's stock price, and increasing stock price is a key task for any manager in a public company. As Diane Primo, chief marketing officer at retailer CDW, observed, "The first thing is, 'How am I going to make money here?'"

Ignoring the profit situation on a business is dangerous. Managers who deliver strong profit results are generally rewarded, and often handsomely; they are promoted, given big bonuses, and awarded prizes. Effort is not the primary criterion for success in business. Hardworking managers who fail to hit profit objectives are generally punished; they receive small bonuses, are passed over for promotions, and are overlooked for prizes. Early on in my career a senior executive at Kraft Foods took me aside and explained, "Good numbers don't guarantee your success, but bad numbers will get you every time." And he was absolutely correct.

A recent global survey of corporate managers highlights the importance of hitting the numbers. The survey looked at the importance of different leadership qualities. The first most respected leadership quality was clear: the "ability to bring in the numbers." This attracted 36 percent of respondents from the United States and Canada. Interpersonal skills, such as influencing and coaching, were second with 15 percent of respondents. Strategic thinking was third with 12 percent. Approximately 4 percent of respondents thought innovation and creativity was most important.[1] A marketing plan needs ideas and creativity, but more than anything, it has to show executives the money. It has to be grounded in the numbers.

The best way to be certain a marketing plan is tied to the numbers is to have a clear financial objective in the plan. As marketer Karen David-Chilowicz explained, "How do you plan a business if you aren't looking at the money coming in and the money going out?" Dell Computer CEO Kevin Rollins observed, "You're in trouble if you don't understand the P&L."[2]

It is almost impossible to create a great marketing plan without a financial objective. Without the full financial picture, the strategic initiatives and tactics don't tie to the overall financial picture of the business, and without a link to the financials, the recommendations lose impact.

A very good way for a marketer to get into trouble is to ignore the financial side of a business. Without a direct link to financials, marketing efforts seem secondary in importance and other things matter more. For example, if marketing efforts are not tied to the P&L, it becomes very easy to cut the spending; without a link, cutting the marketing feels like it will not impact the financial results. Similarly, delaying a key initiative will appear to have no financial ramifications.

This makes marketing vulnerable. As one marketer observed, "This, in my opinion, is the key missing element to many marketing plans. How does it tie to the financials?"

In many companies today, marketing is under fire; people question the effectiveness of marketing efforts and frequently cut the marketing spending. One reason for this is that the role marketing plays in driving the P&L is not clear. As a result, marketing programs are discussed in isolation, and this makes the programs seem optional and discretionary.

The easiest way to make marketing seem optional is to do a marketing plan without a P&L. This is a recipe for disaster.

In the rare circumstances where profit is hard to nail down, or where key profit drivers are clearly beyond the control of the business unit, other financial measures can take the place of absolute profit as a goal in the marketing plan. In the auto industry, for example, costs are driven in large part by commodity pricing and labor rates. Since both of these items are to some extent outside the influence of the marketing team, or even the particular business unit, bottom-line profit is not an ideal goal. A better goal for a business unit, for example, might be revenue less direct costs.

Similarly, the production cost of a feature film is fixed by the time the film hits the theaters. As a result, the marketing plan for the film shouldn't worry too much about the production cost of the film; that is old news. Ticket pricing isn't in direct control of the marketing team; the price of a ticket to customers is set by the individual theaters. In this case, the marketing plan for the film should focus on driving ticket sales and getting people into the theaters to see the movie.

Revenue is a common goal but a flawed one. The advantage of having revenue as a goal in a marketing plan is that the link to marketing efforts is quite clear. Revenue, however, is rarely an ideal goal; in most businesses revenue isn't the problem. Profit is. With enough spending, any business can generate revenue. It might be unprofitable, but the revenue would come in. I could create a business with $10 million in revenue in approximately five minutes; I simply have to sell $20 bills for $19. The sales would come in quickly and last until I ran out of the money and had to shut down.

Other businesses are like this, too. It is not difficult at all to sell pasta at 25 cents a box. However, it is hard to make any profit doing it. It is easy to discount the heck out of something and get some sales. It is hard to make money. As Jim Owens, chairman and CEO of Caterpillar, Inc., observed, "The Holy Grail is not top-line sales growth; it's bottom-line [profit] growth."[3]

Having a profit goal of some sort is a critical part of a marketing plan. As Tropicana's John Bauer explained, "People confuse a marketing plan and a communications plan. If you are not involved in the economics of the business, then all you have is a communications plan."

And the Rest of the Stuff

In many situations, a financial objective is not sufficient on its own; in this case a marketing plan might have one or two other business objectives. These speak to how the plan will be achieved, not just the financial goal.

Most businesses have to balance two forces. The first force is short-term financial pressure; the need to deliver the financial targets. This is critically important for any business. The second force is building a strong, enduring business through creating a differentiated brand and strengthening business capabilities.

Often these two forces fight against each other. Moves to drive short-term profits are frequently harmful to long-term profits.

Examples of this are easy to see. Reducing quality to save a little product cost is a smart move to drive short-term profits, but over the long term it is probably a very bad move, because customers will recognize that quality is eroding. Reducing advertising spending will likely help the short-term financial picture, but it will likely harm the long-term strength of the brand. Launching a new product is expensive; new products usually lose money in the first year. A manager focused solely on a short-term financial target could cut funding for an important long-term new product initiative. By doing so, the manager would increase his or her odds of hitting the short-term target but fail with the new product.

Similarly, moves that build a brand and a strong business may well have a negative impact in the short run. Reducing the amount of discounting on a business will probably strengthen it in the long run by reducing the focus on price as a business driver. The move may well hurt short-term financial results. A major sponsorship program will have a limited short-term impact on sales and will probably hurt short-term profits, but it will strengthen the brand in the long run.

As a result, a financial objective is often insufficient for a business; it suggests the business can focus solely on the financials. This can be dangerous.

This is why many businesses have a broader business goal or two in addition to a financial goal. This broader business goal provides guidance on the "how" in addition to the "what."

For example, a goal such as "Increase market share to 35 percent over the next 12 months" clearly highlights the importance of market share for the business. This is a particularly useful goal for a business that is experiencing fast growth; the business may easily deliver the financial targets while allowing the market share to slide. In the long run, this could be a bad move. Having a market share goal ensures market share is not neglected in the drive for short-term profits.

Similarly, a goal such as "Become one of the top three players in the emerging home-robot category in 12 months" highlights a key growth initiative. By calling out this goal separately, the team keeps the focus on it, despite the fact that it might require a trade-off with the financial target.

The Good, the Bad, and the Ugly

Listed below are objectives from actual marketing plans. Some of these objectives work, and others do not. It is useful to review why.

Beat the Competition
This is not a good objective. It is a good thought, of course. Anyone in business should aspire to beat the competition. The problem is that the objective is very vague. What does that mean?

"Beat the competition" can mean many different things. Does it mean beat the competition in unit market share, dollar marketing share, revenue, or profit? Beat the competition in what market, and what market segment? When will you beat the competition?

In addition, this objective lacks a time element. It isn't clear when the competition will be beaten. An objective like this gives a manager a very easy out: "We'll get there next year."

Increase Operating Profit by 12 Percent versus Previous Year
This is a good objective. It is specific, measurable, and time-specific. It is clear what the target is, and it is simple to determine whether the goal has been achieved or not.

Without knowing the business, it is impossible to assess whether the goal is aggressive or realistic. On the surface, however, a growth of +12 percent seems reasonable for a growing company.

Invest in Quality

This is a not a good objective. It is not specific or measurable, and it has no time element. This objective also isn't aggressive, because investing in quality is easy to do; simply putting $1,000 into improving the package might qualify, but the impact of this move will likely be minimal.

On a more fundamental level, quality is not a great objective on its own. Quality is a means to an end—it isn't an end in itself. The question behind this objective is important: Why invest in quality? What is the goal behind the quality initiative?

It is hard to be opposed to quality, of course, but simply investing in quality is not a good objective.

Achieve Market Share Leadership in the Category by December 2009

This objective is on the right track. It is specific, presumably measurable, and time-specific. It will be clear in 2009 whether the objective has been achieved, and it is possible to measure progress toward the goal.

Of course, it is difficult to assess whether this objective is aggressive or achievable without knowing the starting position and the broader business situation.

Reach $10 Billion in Sales in 2025

This objective has a clear goal and has a time element. The problem is that the objective is far out in the future, so far that it isn't relevant to the issues at hand. If you are creating a plan in 2008, it is best to focus on 2009 and 2010. Looking out 15 years is somewhat pointless; it isn't relevant at all to the questions that need to be addressed in the marketing plan.

It is important to have a long-term vision for a business or course, and to have a sense for where you want to be. But very distant goals should be part of a long-term planning exercise, not a marketing plan.

Objectives are not rallying cries or idle boasts. An objective should be a realistic, pragmatic goal.

Setting Appropriate Expectations

Setting appropriate objectives is more difficult than it might seem. Goals should be high enough to provide motivation but low enough to be realistic and achievable. Gladson CEO Mark Shapiro characterized it this way: "Numbers must be appropriately aggressive yet achievable."

Goals ultimately define success, so it is important to get them right. Is $100 million in profit a good result? Well, if the goal was $120 million, then $100 million is a poor outcome; the team finished well below plan. If the goal was $80 million, however, then $100 million is a terrific outcome; the team far exceeded the objectives.

Some people recommend stretch goals—goals that will be a real challenge to achieve. Better to reach for something and miss, the thinking goes, than shoot too low. If you don't reach for the stars, you won't ever reach them. A very high goal motivates people to do more and achieve more.

This line of thinking is fundamentally flawed. There is nothing wrong with firing up a team with big talking. But exceptionally aggressive goals can create problems. First, high goals set teams up for disappointing results. To achieve the goals, the team must achieve remarkable results, and usually this won't happen. Missing objectives has several negative consequences: employees become discouraged, the sales team may lose motivation, and resources may be shifted to other more "successful" initiatives. According to one marketer, "Adjusting plans downward in midyear can cause inefficiency, loss of credibility, and poor morale." Missing goals also can result in programs being declared unsuccessful, when in reality the program was working fine. This results in rapid changes in programming, which is inefficient.

The other problem with stretch goals is that they can lead to dysfunctional behavior; in an effort to get to the incredibly difficult numbers, people and teams can focus on short-term levers, even if it hurts the business in the long run. If a team can achieve the goals only by burning the furniture, then there is a very real risk this will happen.

In extreme cases, stretch targets and big incentives can motivate employees to engage in unethical or illegal behavior. Bristol-Myers Squibb provides a vivid example of the dangers of high goals. Then-CEO Peter Dolan was a firm believer in setting high goals or as characterized in *Built to Last*, "Big, hairy, audacious goals." So he set high targets and provided big incentives. Under his leadership, a number of senior executives manipulated the timing of product shipments to overstate short-term results; the company shipped product to distributors at the end of a fiscal year and booked the revenue, thereby apparently delivering strong results. In reality, of course, the sales were meaningless; they were simply pulled forward. Between 1999 and 2001, the company overstated revenues by $2.5 billion to meet quarterly sales targets.[4]

Objectives must reflect balance. As one marketing executive explained, good objectives are feasible: "They are relevant, they are doable, and they don't reach too far."

THE BIG MOVES: STRATEGIC INITIATIVES

The most important element of any great plan is the strategic initiatives. Although a plan is built to achieve objectives (and the objectives must be set first), the heart of a plan, and the most important part, is the strategic initiatives.

The strategic initiatives are precisely what the business will do to achieve the objectives. These are the big ideas; they set the direction. As a result, this section should be the focus for people creating a plan and for people reviewing a plan. Strategic initiatives are the heart of the matter.

A strategic initiative is an action. Strategic initiatives are the big, broad moves that will help the business achieve the objectives. Strategic initiatives are much like strategies, and the phrases can be used somewhat interchangeably. However, I like to use the term strategic initiative better than strategy, because the phrase makes it clear that the focus is on action. When people think strategy, there is a tendency to think big, abstract thoughts that have very little to do with what the business will be doing over the next 12 months.

The most important thing to remember is that strategic initiatives are the actions. They are not the intended final outcome; that is the objective. They are not the tactical recommendation; that is the tactic. The strategy is the overall action. As noted in *The Marketing Plan*, "An objective is what you want to achieve. A strategy is how you plan to achieve your objectives."[5]

No Time for Philosophy

Philosophy is a wonderful thing. It is good to think big thoughts and ponder on the meaning of life and other profound issues. It is also important; the big issues really do matter.

Big thoughts are also important when running a business. Long-term strategy is a good topic for consideration. Values really do matter. Principles, too, play an important role in shaping a business.

However, the strategic initiatives in a marketing plan are not the place for philosophical considerations. A strategic initiative should be precise and action-oriented. It should clearly state what needs to be done.

A good strategic initiative has several characteristics. First, it should be clear. The statement should state in obvious language precisely what is to be done. Second, a strategic initiative should be action-oriented; it is, after all, an initiative. There should be a verb in the phrase. Third, a good strategic initiative should be measurable, so that it is possible to evaluate whether headway is being made against the initiative or not. Fourth, a strategic initiative should directly support the objectives; there has to be linkage across the plan.

"Increase sales with heaviest users" could be a good strategic initiative. It is clear, action-oriented, measurable, and presumably in support of the objectives.

Similarly, "attract new customers to the category" is a good strategic initiative. It is clear and direct. It is very possible to measure progress. A team could easily develop tactics to support the initiative. Of course, the tactics would be completely different from the tactics for the heavy user effort mentioned earlier. That is why strategic initiatives are important.

"Innovation" is not a good strategic initiative. Certainly, innovation is a good thing; it is virtually impossible to be against it. Opposing innovation is a bit like opposing the environment; you really can't be opposed to it. But on its own, innovation is just a word. It doesn't really say anything. What sort of innovation are we talking about? What is the action that will be involved?

Is this a new product? Or is this a new cash management system? Or is this a way to produce products for less?

Empty words lead to enormous problems. They sound good and seem to make sense. Who isn't in favor of innovation? What, you don't support innovation? Are you crazy? Are you stuck in the mud? The problem is that the empty words don't actually say anything at all.

"Differentiate through added value" is another flawed strategy. It is action-oriented, which is good. But it is terribly, hopelessly vague. It doesn't really say anything at all. What is the way to differentiate? What type of added value is being considered? As one marketer observed about this strategy, "It can mean a million different things."

"Run a coupon good for 30 cents off on August 4" is also not a good strategic initiative. It is simply a tactic. Although the phrase is clear, precise, and measurable, it is purely descriptive of a tactical marketing move. There is probably a larger initiative behind this tactic, but it isn't readily apparent what it might be. To flesh out the real strategic initiative, the questions to ask are simple: What do we hope to accomplish with the coupon? Why are we doing this, anyway? How will it build sales?

It may be that the intent of the coupon is to get trial on a new product. In this case, the strategic initiative might be "Drive trial on the new product" or even broader "Launch new product."

"Quality" is not a strategic initiative. Much like innovation, quality is a very good thing. It is hard to be against quality. But the word quality on its own says nothing. Is this about improving product quality? Or is this about reducing product quality? What is the action? What is the point? A better strategic initiative based on quality would be "improve service experience" or "address quality concerns."

THE POWER OF THREE

The inherent challenge in identifying strategic initiatives is that you can only have a few. If you could have two dozen initiatives, things would be simple. Indeed, most businesses would have pretty much the same exact list, highlighting everything one can do with a business. Things get difficult because a business can only focus on a few things.

The best number of strategic initiatives for a business is three. This is true whether the business is small or large; the best number is three.

Having three strategic initiatives provides two benefits. First, it forces great focus, and focus is essential for getting things done. The truth is that although we like to think we can do lots of things at the same time, we can't. As Adobe's Mark Delman observed, "You can only get an organization to do a couple things in any given year." AspireUp's Roland Jacobs is also a believer in the power of three, noting, "Even the most complex business should have three things it's focused on."

Second, it is easy to communicate and remember three things. People tend to remember things in groups of threes and fours. This, of course, is why many phone numbers around the globe are broken into groups of three and four numbers. Three is easy to grasp and understand.

It is possible to have four strategic initiatives, or even five, and to still retain some focus. Each additional initiative, however, subtracts from the overall impact of the plan.

Eight strategic initiatives are too many; they are just a list of things to do. It is impossible to focus on eight things. The same is true for 11, 14, and 17; the complexity is too great. As one executive observed, "You can't have 13."

Having just one or two initiatives is also not good, because it doesn't provide much texture. If a business has just one or two strategic initiatives, then they are most likely very broad and general. For example, a company that outlines the two initiatives of "build revenues" and "build margins" isn't saying very much at all; the strategic initiatives are all-encompassing; almost everything falls into one bucket or the other. Similarly, a plan with the initiatives of "build sales with existing customers" and "build sales with new customers" is adding very little value; it would be simpler to say, "build sales," because the two broad strategic initiatives include everyone, anyway.

Researchers at Eli Lilly recently completed a study that highlighted the importance of communicating just a few things. The Lilly study looked at the communication of drug side effects. What happened, the researchers wondered, as a company communicated more side effects about a drug? Would people actually remember more? Or was being thorough and including more side effects actually counterproductive, so that people remembered fewer?

In the study, the researchers created three different versions of the same print ad. One version of the ad included 4 side effects, another version of the ad included 8 side effects, and the final version of the ad included 12 side effects. The researchers then showed the ads to consumers and evaluated what people remembered.

Surprisingly, the study showed that increasing the number of side effects in the ad did not result in consumers remembering more. Instead, the reverse happened; increasing the number of side effects in the ad meant that people actually remembered fewer. Consumers on average remembered 1.04 side effects when shown an ad that listed 4 side effects, and consumers remembered only 0.85 side effects when shown an ad with 12 side effects. This suggests that when people see more information they remember less on a percentage basis, and less in the absolute.

In addition, as the number of side effects listed in the ad increased, more and more people failed to remember any of them at all. With 4 side effects, 36 percent of consumers couldn't remember even 1. With 8 side effects, the portion of consumers who couldn't remember any of them increased to 45 percent. With 12 side effects, a remarkable 53 percent of consumers could not remember even one of the side effects. This suggests that the more data people see, the more likely they are to forget everything.[6]

Of course, this really is just common sense. Long lists of things are difficult; people quickly get overwhelmed and forget everything. Recently,

I went to a talk on the 11 keys to successful branding. The talk was quite interesting, and the speaker had some very good points. However, after the talk I couldn't remember any of the points; there were so many different things to keep track of, I lost track of them all. I had to go back to my notes to remember the list. And then, when I was later asked about the talk, I was able to recall only a few things.

A marketing plan should never have a dozen initiatives. This indicates a lack of focus. More importantly, the plan will not be memorable. The audience is likely to simply be overwhelmed, and this is not a positive.

Having 10 strategic initiatives is perhaps the worst of all. It is too many for people to remember, and the number is so round and even that it seems like the plan was simply stretched or compressed to make things neat and tidy.

Paring down and focusing on three strategic initiatives is difficult, but this is the heart of the marketing plan process, and it is the process that will help bring your company the most success. Indeed, if you're not able to distill the plan down into the most important strategies, the work isn't done. One executive noted that getting down to three strategies is critical, explaining, "If you can't focus it that much, you don't really have a strategy."

Developing strategic initiatives is the heart of the marketing plan process. This phase is where the team adds the most value; identifying the most important things for a business to focus on is tough work. It is the manager's best opportunity to influence the business.

Strategic initiatives come from analysis and from thinking. A manager must be able to take all the information available and distill it down into the most important factors. As Nestlé's Steven Cunliffe observed, "You need to be able to synthesize a lot of material and turn it into some logical strategies."

THE BIG EVENTS:
BRING ON THE TACTICS

Tactics are the specifics: the programs and ideas that will bring the broader strategies to life. The tactics lay out precisely what will be done. A strategy sets the overall direction, and the tactic provides the specific execution point. Put another way, the strategies highlight what needs to happen, and the tactics show how precisely it will happen.

Tactics include advertising campaigns, promotions, sponsorships, and product improvements. Tactics are sales efforts, public relations campaigns, and Internet marketing efforts. They are the details, the actions, and the meat.

For example, Nike might pursue the strategic initiative, gain share, and establish credibility in soccer. The tactics supporting this initiative could include identifying and sponsoring promising young soccer stars, introducing a new line of high-end soccer footwear, and expanding retail presence of the soccer line.

Of course, only the most important tactics should be highlighted in a marketing plan; the goal is to focus on the most critical things. Every product has a price, for example, but pricing should only show up in a marketing plan if pricing is particularly important as a tactic.

Every strategic initiative should have tactics. Indeed, an initiative without tactics is a red flag; if an initiative doesn't have specific actions associated with it, odds are that nothing will happen. The intent is there, but the action is not.

Similarly, each tactic should be connected to a broader strategic initiative. There should be a direct connection between a strategy and a tactic. For any tactic, the questions that have to be asked are simple: Why are we doing this? What strategic initiative does it support?

If a tactic isn't connected to an initiative, a manager should take a second look at the tactic. Is the tactic really that important? And if it is important, why is that the case? What is the initiative behind the tactic? Is there really another strategic initiative the tactic is driving? If so, should this replace one of the ones currently highlighted in the plan?

Being disciplined about linking tactics to strategic initiatives is a fundamental key to success. It is through the process of focusing on the most important tactics that a plan takes life. As J&J's Sharon D'Agostino observed, "The key is being relentless in doing just what you say you're going to do. If it isn't consistent with the strategy, we aren't going to do it."

The 4 Ps at Last

Tactics are where the familiar 4 Ps should appear in a marketing plan. The 4 Ps, of course, include product, pricing, promotion, and place (or distribution). Generally, these issues will be addressed specifically in the tactics section of a marketing plan.

In most cases, the 4 Ps are not strategic initiatives. Promotion alone is rarely a strategic initiative; promotion is a means to accomplish something specific, which will in turn drive sales. For example, a coupon might be focused on driving trial on a new product, and this supports the overall objective of building revenue and profit. Similarly, distribution programs need to be viewed in the larger context; a distribution drive is usually done to achieve something specific, which will ultimately drive sales and profit.

Anyone who looks upon the 4 Ps as strategic initiatives in and of themselves is likely to encounter problems; the plan will end up being very tactical, lacking integration across the different elements.

For example, if overall goals are to drive profit and share growth, a strategic initiative might be to attract competitors' customers. The tactics supporting this initiative might then span the 4 Ps. For example, one tactic might be using advertising to encourage people to compare the products

(Promotion). Another tactic could be cutting prices to match competition (Price). Another might be to expand distribution in key geography (Place).

*   *   *

A marketing plan really needs just three things. The first is the goals and objectives, or what the business is trying to achieve. The second is the strategic initiatives, or the three or four big moves the business will make in order to achieve growth. The third is the tactics, or the specific programs and moves that the business will make to support the strategic initiatives. It really is strikingly simple.

CHAPTER 4

The Best of the Best

While researching this book, I asked dozens of marketers the same question: "Think about the best marketing plan you have ever seen. What made it so good?" The answers were remarkably consistent. It didn't matter whether the person worked in pharmaceuticals, financial services, or consumer packaged goods. It didn't matter whether the person worked for a nonprofit or a for-profit organization in the United States or Asia. The answers were all basically the same.

It isn't entirely surprising that what works in one industry works in another, because marketing plans are always about people, both externally (customers) and internally (the business team and senior management). And people are people.

The best marketing plans have four things in common, and these four traits can be summarized by the acronym FACS: They are focused, achievable, compelling, and simple.

IT IS FOCUSED: "WE KNOW EXACTLY WHERE WE'RE GOING"

Focus is the most important characteristic of good marketing; a great plan concentrates on the most important initiatives and the most important tactics.

The challenge for managers today isn't to identify things that are good to do or things that would help grow sales. That is a fairly simple task. The challenge is picking the few things that will really matter, the things that will have a major impact on the business.

Great plans highlight the most important priorities for the business and don't get bogged down by including everything. The best marketing plans will embrace focus. The plan will highlight what has to happen, why it is important, and how it will occur.

For most businesses, there are just a few things that really matter at any given point. There are many details to manage, of course. Shipments have to go out, supplies have to be ordered, customers have to be billed, and taxes have to be paid. But success, or failure, will stem from just a few big initiatives.

Understanding this is essential; a manager who knows that just a few things really matter can focus intensely on those things.

Dell Computer founder Michael Dell credits much of his company's success to developing strong business plans with focus. He observed in a 2005 interview, "For the past decade, we've identified three major objectives every year—the same initiatives, supported by the same metrics, everywhere in the world." He continued, "A lot of our success is due to the fact that we've been able to pick the right things at the right time and align the entire worldwide organization around them. They help the entire organization stay focused on what we're trying to accomplish...."[1] Jeff Immelt, CEO of General Electric, echoed the thought. Immelt noted in a 2004 interview, "Every leader needs to clearly explain the top three things the organization is working on. If you can't, then you're not leading well."[2]

Marketing plans should operate at a high level, with a focus on the big strategic initiatives and then the most important tactics. Indeed, it is easy to get bogged down in the tactical details of the plan. Tactics are easy to talk about; there are all sorts of interesting things to say about any particular promotion or pricing plan. Indeed, it is great fun to present the ins and outs of a new and exciting program. Even the most mundane of marketing tactics, a coupon in the Sunday morning paper, can lead to all sorts of interesting, thought-provoking, and sometimes controversial discussions. What is the value of the coupon? Should it be good off two, or good off one? When will it run? When do you expect the competitors to have coupons? Do you want to be before them, or after? How much time until the coupon expires? Why? What products will be featured in the picture? What color is the background?

The problem, of course, is that all these questions are relatively unimportant. Tactical plans tend to be long, detailed, and ultimately not productive. The big issues are never addressed, and the tactical questions and issues dominate the discussion. Instead of talking about the growth drivers of the business, or ways to deal with a major competitive threat, a tactical marketing plan wastes time on small, unimportant programs, such as the sampling program in Omaha or the PR event in Frankfurt. It misses the point.

The process of focusing is difficult because the marketer must filter and prioritize, including only the recommendations and data that truly have an impact on the business. As James Kilts, former CEO of Nabisco and Gillette observed, "Regardless of your position in a company or organization, there is always a flood of information and data, and a lot of conflicting ideas and opinions. In the end, how you get to the heart of the matter will define you as a leader."[3]

Focusing is challenging, because the world is full of interesting and relevant information. Of course, people filter all the time. Barry Schwartz, author of *The Paradox of Choice*, observed that cutting out irrelevant information is something people do all the time. According to Schwartz, "Filtering out extraneous information is one of the basic functions of consciousness. If everything available to our senses demanded our attention at all times, we wouldn't be able to get through the day."[4] Marketing plans are similar; if an executive included all the possible details in a plan, no one would ever be able to read it.

Marketing veterans consistently point to focus as a key to great marketing plans. Conagra's Sergio Pereira points out that focused plans show that the manager knows the business. He says, "A great plan makes it easy to tell that people have figured out the things that matter and the things that don't."

It Is Achievable: "We Can Do That"

At one point in my career, I was promoted to run a dynamic new business. The business had just ended its second year in the market, a year marked by sharp increases in sales volume and market share. After meeting the team, I sat down to review the marketing plan for the business, and I was rather dismayed at what I read.

I quickly realized that the business had been growing quickly due to very high levels of spending in both advertising and promotions. The business's top-selling item, a nondifferentiated item, was stealing share due to all the promotion activity on the business.

The marketing plan for the following year called for further growth in share and sales but a sharp reduction in spending. The theory was that after two years of introductory support, the business had enough momentum to continue growing in year three in the market.

The problem, of course, was that the marketing plan was not at all based on reality. Cutting promotion support on a product that sold mainly due to the high levels of promotion was not going to result in continued growth. Instead, the business would collapse.

The marketing plan, in other words, was a purely fictional document built on either a lack of understanding or, as it turned out, a heavy dose of wishful thinking. It was totally unachievable.

A great marketing plan has to be built on realistic assumptions. It has to be achievable on the basis of the dynamics in the market. A marketing plan built on unrealistic assumptions is worth nothing. It is a bit like doing a financial plan based on winning the lottery; it all looks great but is not likely to happen. As Barry Sternlicht, former chairman and CEO of Starwood Hotels and Resorts Worldwide noted, "When you start making decisions based on what you wish were true, you're going to make some pretty bad calls."[5]

In a strong marketing plan, objectives are achievable, the strategic initiatives are feasible, and the tactics are believable. In total, the plan has to pass the sniff test; it has to be credible.

Achievability is why every marketing plan should have a section on financials; it is an essential piece of a good plan. Financials play a critical role in the planning process. As Unilever veteran David Hirschler stated, "The financials are the most important part."

Ultimately, a marketing plan has to work financially. The spending on the business has to drive sufficient revenue to deliver the needed profit. In particular, there should be a clear link between the recommended strategic initiatives and the financials. If the business succeeds at executing the initiatives, will the business deliver the financial targets? Why or why not? One marketing leader explained the situation by saying, "It is one thing to say you want to grow 10 percent a year. It is another to really understand how you will get there."

To show how a business *will* get there, a marketing plan should include basic, realistic financial projections, showing the outlook for the business and how the strategies will translate into results. This is essential to ensure that the marketing plan will deliver the needed objectives. As one general manager observed, "I can't imagine a marketing plan without a P&L. It's theory without the P&L."

Ignoring the financial outlook for a business is an enormous miss; it ignores the key objective and doesn't highlight how the recommended strategies and tactics link to the results. As Tropicana's John Bauer explained, "The P&L links the spending to the business."

As important as financials are to a great marketing plan, managers should be clear that a marketing plan is not a budget, and it shouldn't be confused with the development of an annual budget. Getting lost in financial calculations is a common pitfall for marketing plans. As Quaker veteran Mark Shapiro noted, "Every time a business gets hung up in its financials, it's a problem."

It Is Compelling: "Makes Sense to Me"

A great marketing plan is compelling; someone reading or hearing the plan should walk away convinced that the recommendations make sense and are the best available. This is essential. Since a primary goal of a marketing plan is to gain support, the plan must be convincing to be successful. Stephen Cunliffe, president of the frozen foods division at Nestlé USA, has reviewed hundreds of marketing plans over the course of his career. He observed that great plans leave a reviewer feeling comfortable with the plan and the team. He says, "These guys know where they're going, and I have confidence."

Many marketing plans fall short in this area. The plan explains what needs to be done, but the plan doesn't explain how it will work. It isn't convincing.

To be convincing, a plan must explain why the recommendations make sense. It also must highlight why the objectives are correct and why the strategies will work to achieve the objectives.

A plan also must proactively deal with potential questions or issues. A great marketing plan highlights alternative strategies and why they will not work as well as the plan's final recommendation. A marketer writing an excellent plan anticipates obvious questions and proactively answers them.

To be compelling, a plan needs to be based on data and analysis. Facts are facts, and they provide reason for someone to believe in the recommendation. In a sense, facts are the foundation on which a great marketing plan is built.

It Is Simple: "Whew. That Was Easy"

Great marketing plans are simple. The issues are apparent, the strategies make sense, and the tactics clearly show the execution of the strategies. The rationale supports the points. It is clear why the data is being presented and what it means.

The most successful marketing plans have a flow; the facts fit together, the points flow logically from one to the next, the strategies build to tactics and to the financial implications. It all feels simple and intuitive. Someone reading the plan might say, "Well, of course. This is obviously what we should be doing. It won't be easy, but the plan makes sense."

Simplicity is important, since one of the main reasons managers write marketing plans is to get approval and support for their recommendation. Before someone can support something, of course, they have to understand it. A simple plan, then, is critical to gain support.

It is tempting to think that complicated and data-intensive plans are most likely to receive support. If I include everything, some people seem to think, others will see all the information and agree with my conclusion. This is flawed thinking. If people can't understand the plan, or they can't follow the analysis or even don't manage to finish reading the plan, they are not likely to support it.

Most businesses are fundamentally simple. The strategies that drive businesses are not difficult to follow. Businesses only become complex when the details are added. As General Electric's Jack Welch observed, "People always over-estimate how complex business is. This isn't rocket science; we've chosen one of the world's more simple professions. Most global businesses have three or four critical competitors, and you know who they are. And there aren't that many things you can do with a business. It's not as if you're choosing among 2,000 options."[6]

Recent academic research studies have shown the importance of simplicity. Two of the more interesting studies were conducted by Sheena Iyengar and Mark Lepper and published in the *Journal of Personality and Social Psychology*.

In the first study, Iyengar and Lepper sampled high-end jam in a grocery store; they set up a table in the store and invited people to sample different jams. At certain times, they offered six different jams to consumers. At other times, the pair offered 24 different jams.

The results were striking. When more jams were offered, more people stopped to try the jam (60 percent versus 40 percent), which indicated that a larger selection was initially more appealing. However, few people who stopped ultimately purchased a jam when forced to decide between 24 different options. Only 3 percent of the people who stopped at the table with 24 different jams purchased a jam. Conversely, almost 30 percent of the people who stopped at the table with six different jams ultimately purchased. The results seemed to contradict common sense; people should embrace options and choice.

The key insight, however, is that more isn't always better. Twenty-four jams were simply too many; consumers were overwhelmed by the selection and couldn't make a decision, and so they walked away without making a purchase.

In another study, Iyengar and Lepper had consumers taste Godiva chocolate. Participants could choose from either 6 or 30 different varieties. Iyengar and Lepper then studied how well the consumers liked the chocolate and simulated a purchase by letting participants choose between money and chocolate in return for participating in the study.

Once again, the results were clear and counterintuitive. Consumers who chose between fewer chocolates generally liked the chocolate better (average satisfaction of 6.3 versus 5.5), and they were more inclined to ultimately purchase the chocolate by choosing the chocolate instead of the money (48 percent versus 12 percent). Tellingly, consumers who chose between the 30 chocolates later had a sense of regret about the experience.[7]

The research by Iyengar and Lepper highlights the importance of simplicity. Making things complicated often makes them less appealing. More data isn't better, more choice isn't better, and more options aren't better. The key is simplicity. A great marketing plan takes all the data and all the research and boils it down into the key initiatives. As Tropicana's John Bauer observed, "It's all about synthesizing the data to find the relevant information."

*   *   *

The characteristics of a great marketing plan are universal; they are focused, achievable, compelling, and simple (FACS). Anyone creating a marketing plan should test the plan against these simple criteria. Before presenting a plan, look at it and ask a few basic questions. Is this plan focused on just a few big things? Can we really achieve the goals? Is it presented in a compelling way? Is it simple to read and understand?

Asking these basic questions will ensure the plan is on the right track.

CHAPTER 5

The Road Map: Step by Step

Marketing plans don't just appear. Creating a breakthrough marketing plan takes time, energy, and effort. You can't just sit down and write a marketing plan in an hour, unless you are working in a very small organization and already know the business exceptionally well. A good plan is based on a deep understanding of the business, the customer, the competition, and the market, smart strategic thinking, and solid program development. All of this takes time.

It can be difficult to know where to start, because in almost every case there are many issues to address and piles and piles of data to work with. The questions, and the potential solutions, go on and on and on.

Starting in the wrong spot can lead to trouble. Action-oriented people will tend to begin the marketing plan process by thinking about tactical moves and specific programs. "We need a new advertising campaign!" they may exclaim as they kick off the process. Or, "We should run our summer promotion early this year to preempt the competition!" This is a tempting approach, but it is rarely successful. Specific tactical decisions, such as advertising spending, packaging changes, and the timing of promotions, should be made only once the overall plan is clear. For example, it makes little sense to talk about advertising creative until there is an agreement on the role and purpose of advertising in the overall plan.

Thoughtful, analytic people may begin the marketing planning process by studying the business and understanding the ins and outs of the market; they will look at recent results, trends, competitive moves, changes in the channel, and consumer shifts. This approach is conceptually fine; a good plan should be grounded in analysis. It is hard to argue against analysis. But starting with analysis frequently leads to problems, too; the amount of analysis one can do on a business is virtually unlimited, so there is a very real risk that the entire process will get bogged down in this step and nothing will ever get done.

Creating a good marketing plan requires a road map; a step-by-step approach where each step in the process is important and where each step should be completed before things move on to the next step.

This chapter presents an eight-step process for creating a breakthrough marketing plan that is appropriate for both small and large businesses. It will be your roadmap to success in creating your own breakthrough marketing plan.

STEP 1: CREATE
A CROSS-FUNCTIONAL TEAM

It is impossible to create a marketing plan without cross-functional involvement. This fact was highlighted for me several years ago when I sat in on the annual plan presentation for a $500 million business. The category director was enthusiastic and delighted with her team's plan.

At the end of the two-hour meeting, she wrapped up with a big, high-energy finish: "We are incredibly excited about this plan and think we have a terrific year ahead. Thank you for your time and attention. Now the team will be happy to take your questions!"

The room fell silent for a minute, while the audience digested all the material. Then, from the back, came the first comment. It was from the vice president of sales. "This is all well and good, but it won't work, you know. You can't reallocate trade spending across markets; we have too many national accounts to do that."

The category director paused, and then commented, "But reallocating trade spending lets us reduce our spending, and this in turn lets us invest in the additional advertising we are counting on to build the brand."

The vice president of sales frowned. "I understand what you want to do. I'm just saying you can't do it. It won't work."

And with that, a hush fell over the room.

"Why don't we take this off-line?" said the category director, seizing the one emergency rip cord available. It was the only possible way out. But the energy from the presentation was gone, and everyone in the audience knew it. The category director had failed to involve critical people in the decision making process during the writing of the marketing plan, and as a result the entire plan was built on incorrect assumptions.

Creating a marketing plan is a cross-functional activity. It is impossible to write a marketing plan in isolation. The decisions in a marketing plan are cross-functional in nature; they have an impact on marketing, marketing research, sales, R&D, human resources, finance, and almost every other function in a company. As a result, many functions have to provide input and, ultimately, agree with the plan and the recommendations.

In many cases, a particular person or department will be responsible for leading the planning process; this might be the brand manager, the marketing vice president, or even the general manager. Having a clear leader is important, because ownership is essential; someone has to drive things forward. This does not negate the fact that broad involvement is essential.

As a result, the first step in developing a marketing plan is simple but frequently overlooked: assemble the cross-functional team that will create and own the plan.

There are two reasons to start by creating a cross-functional team. First, this will lead to a better plan. A good marketing plan will touch all parts of a business and consider issues that directly affect almost every function. This includes new products, advertising, pricing, sales, customer service, public relations, quality control, and production planning. The list goes on and on. A marketing plan that doesn't at least think about R&D efforts, for example, will be less than optimal. Similarly, a plan that doesn't consider product quality and product cost will be incomplete.

As a result, it is essential to involve the cross-functional team in the marketing plan process. It is very hard to discuss issues related to the sales force, for example, without involvement from the sales organization. It is similarly difficult to discuss new product development without the participation of the R&D group. Cross-functional team members bring insights, knowledge, and ideas. If it is impossible to implement a packaging change, for example, it's best to know this early in the process.

Indeed, if the only people working on a marketing plan are the people who work in marketing, then there is a problem. The final product will fall far short of its potential; it will either only address core marketing topics such as advertising and promotions or not have the needed information.

The second reason to form a cross-functional team is to build support. There is no better way to gain someone's support than to involve them in the decision making process. It's easy to criticize a plan you didn't create. It's hard to criticize a plan you created; if there were problems, why didn't you address them?

Indeed, excluding a particularly influential player from the marketing planning process entirely is a big risk; they may well find fault later. More significantly, they may feel excluded, and even angry. This is dangerous—it's easy to find fault with any marketing plan if you start with that goal.

In the unfortunate story earlier, it is very clear that the sales group was not involved in creating the plan. As a result, the plan was based on an assumption about trade spending that was fundamentally and fatally flawed.

Importantly, having the functions represented is not enough; you have to be careful to get the right people. This is a bit of an art. Having senior people on the team is good because they bring knowledge and insight. Frequently, however, they will not have time to fully participate in the process; they will miss meetings and never fully engage in the project. Junior people may have more time and motivation, but they may lack the necessary credibility. Balance is important; you need people with enough experience to contribute, but you also need people who are willing and able to spend time on the task.

When creating the team, a leader should identify the key players, gather them together, lay out the plan, and secure commitment to the task.

In reality, not every member of the team will be equally involved; some are there to provide input and give buy-in rather than to take the lead at writing the plan. Nonetheless, involving people early and often will ensure that the final plan deals with obvious issues and has cross-functional support.

STEP 2: CHECK THE FOUNDATION

You can't build a strong house on a weak foundation, and the same is true for a marketing plan; you can't create a breakthrough marketing plan if the fundamentals are not in place. Before you can develop a marketing plan, you need to understand what the business is built on in the first place.

As a result, the second step in the process is to check the foundation of the business to confirm the long-term direction. This step is often just a routine check, to ensure that the foundation is still solid and strong. Sometimes, however, it becomes clear that there is no foundation, or that it is unstable. In this case there is more work to do—but not on the marketing plan.

Marketing plans are by nature relatively short-term vehicles; the focus is on the next one, two, or, at most, three years. Marketing plans are not long-term strategic planning documents; a marketing plan should address what the business will do in the immediate future. A marketing plan with a 10-year horizon is so broad and vague that it does little to address the immediate questions of what should be done now and why.

Brands and business, however, have a much longer horizon. Brands can live for decades or centuries or, perhaps, forever. Ford was founded in 1903. Gucci started in 1921. Coke first appeared in 1886. Starbucks, though it seems like an overnight success story, dates back to 1970.

Indeed, most of the value of a business lies far in the future; the next one or two years are important, but what really matters is the next decade, and the decade after that. Simply looking at a basic net present value calculation highlights this; if you use a 5 percent discount rate and value a business that produces a flat stream of cash flows, you quickly realize that the next year accounts for only 5 percent of the value of the business. The value lies in the future.

As a result, the marketing plan process has to be created with a sense of the larger picture. Any decision on a business has to be made with an appreciation of the long term; this provides context. Decisions in the next one or two years have to move the organization toward its long-term goal and build on the past.

By reviewing the core direction of a business up front, the team can understand the longer-term objectives and developing opportunities. In addition, understanding the foundation of the business lowers the risk that the final plan will be inconsistent with the long-term direction of the organization.

For example, deciding to increase prices at Wal-Mart might appear to be a sound idea to increase margins and profits. However, the Wal-Mart brand is built entirely on value; if prices increase, then the entire brand positioning changes. Similarly, deciding to launch a high-performance convertible might be a way for Volvo to drive incremental sales, but the move would be inconsistent with Volvo's core positioning of safety. This would make little sense.

There are two things in particular to look at in this stage of the process: positioning and vision. These are quite different, and both are important. Positioning defines what a brand means. Vision describes what an organization hopes to achieve in the long run; it provides a sense of purpose and the big picture.

Every business should have a vision and a brand positioning. These are two basic, fundamental tools. It is hard to lead an organization without an understanding of its long-term goals, and it is hard to manage a brand without understanding the positioning.

In most cases, this step in the marketing plan process is simply a process of assembling the materials. Both vision and positioning should remain fairly constant from year to year, so the focus should not be changing either document unless absolutely necessary.

However, if one or the other doesn't exist or is clearly off, this step becomes more complicated and will require some work. It is time well spent, because setting a strong foundation for the marketing plan is critically important. A house built on a weak foundation may look nice while it is being built, but it will ultimately crumble. Similarly, a marketing plan built without a sense of the bigger picture will usually miss the mark.

Positioning

A brand is a set of associations linked to a name, mark, or symbol. A brand is everything that pops into your head when you think of a product. When you think about BMW, for example, you may think of performance, technology, Germany, and expensive. When you think about McDonald's, you may think of kids, French fries, quick, golden arches, and hamburgers.

The difference between a name and a brand is simple. A name has no associations. It is simply a name. For example, Claire's Cola doesn't mean a lot. It is simply a name. Coca-Cola, however, has all sorts of associations, making it a brand.

Brands matter because people never just see a product; they see a product and a brand. The brand functions as a lens that changes how people see the product. People see the product specifications, of course, but these are shaped by the brand. Vodka, a colorless, odorless, and tasteless liquid, becomes very special when the Grey Goose brand is applied to it. In the United States, a perfectly fine automobile may take on negative quality associations when it is linked with General Motors.

Great marketers understand that shaping the associations around a brand is a key business challenge. A strong brand will help a product for many, many years. A weak brand will hurt for just as long.

Positioning is an essential tool for managing a brand. It is grounded in a very simple insight: great brands are tightly defined. The best brands stand for something distinct. In automobiles, Volvo stands for safety, BMW stands for performance, Rolls-Royce stands for luxury, and Toyota stands for durable quality.

It is impossible for a brand to be all things to all people. Indeed, the more a brand tries to appeal to everyone, the more the brand loses what makes it distinct; in an effort to broaden its appeal, a brand becomes more and more general.

Brand positioning is a tool for clarifying how a brand will compete in the market; it states the intended meaning for a brand. Ideally, a brand positioning is the same as the associations in the market. Sometimes there is a disconnect between the two; the company wants the brand to mean something, but it actually means something else. This highlights the need for more work to ensure that the brand means what the company wants it to mean.

There are four essential parts to a brand positioning: target, frame of reference, primary benefit, and key attribute.

The first part of a positioning is target or who the brand is for. This is usually on the basis of a market segmentation study. It is almost always grounded in a deep insight into the customer. A brand can't appeal to everyone. Importantly, the target in a positioning does not need to include everyone who buys the brand; it should simply specify who the brand is for.

The second part is the frame of reference or what the brand really is. This can be thought of as the competitive set. Sometimes this is obvious. Steinway, for example, is a brand of high-end piano. McDonald's is a fast-food restaurant. Grey Goose is a brand of vodka. Sometimes, though, this question is less obvious. What, precisely, is Yahoo? Having a clear frame of reference is important; it is hard to explain to someone why to buy something if you don't first tell them what it is.

The third part of a positioning is the primary benefit or the most important reason for the target to buy the product. The key thing to remember when it comes to positioning is that a brand can have only one benefit. Brands that try to be many things all at the same time end up causing confusion.

The final part of the positioning is the reason why. This should support the primary benefit; the reason why provides the evidence points that justifies the positioning. A brand can have one or two or even three reasons why. All of them, however, should support the positioning.

The four elements of a positioning can be presented in a simple statement that combines all the parts. The statement follows a simple format.

To (target),
x is the brand of (frame of reference)
that (primary benefit)
because (key attributes).

A brand positioning statement should work as a single thought. The target should value the benefit. The benefit should be relevant and differentiating within the frame of reference. The reasons why should support the benefit.

When written out, a brand positioning can look something like this.

To serious athletes,
Nike is the brand of athletic equipment and apparel
that lets you perform your very best
because Nike products are made with the latest and best technology and design.

To people who know and appreciate fine coffee,
Peet's is the brand of premium coffee
that has the most robust taste
because Peet's is roasted daily by people who are passionate about coffee.

A positioning statement is not a slogan; it is a tool to be used internally to help define the intended meaning of a brand. It feels clunky when written out, in a self-conscious sort of way. But a positioning statement is a powerful way to summarize what a brand means.

In addition to a positioning statement, a brand may also have a brand character statement. A brand character statement describes the personality of the brand. Positioning is how a brand competes with other players in the market. Brand character is the spirit of the brand.

If brand positioning is all about differentiation, brand character is all about personality. It is not necessary for a brand character to be unique. But a brand character should capture the spirit of the brand. For example, the Tiffany brand character might include words such as classic, elegant, refined, traditional, and romantic.

Importantly, every brand should have a positioning. If an organization has 12 different brands, there should be 12 different positioning statements and 12 brand character statements.

Vision

Vision sets the long-term direction for a business; it speaks to the big question of what an organization wants to achieve in the long run. In a sense, vision answers the age-old question, "So what do you want to be when you grow up?" As Jim Collins and Jerry Porras wrote in their classic 1996 article on vision, "Companies that enjoy enduring success have core values and a core purpose that remain fixed while their business strategies and practices endlessly adapt to a changing world."[1]

It is highly unlikely that a series of one- or two-year plans will lead a business to its long-term goal. A company that wants to be the quality leader may or may not actually achieve this if the business team simply focuses just on optimizing plans for the next year. Each year, for example, the focus might be on using promotions to drive volume and cost reductions to prop up profits. This plan might deliver some solid financial results, at least in the short run. But the plan certainly won't achieve the long-term objective.

As a result, a business team needs to approach a marketing plan with a sense of the greater goal and the greater purpose. The marketing plan then needs to build toward the long-term goals.

There are three particularly important things to consider when formulating a vision. The first is the statement of purpose or what the organization actually does. For example, according to Procter & Gamble CEO A.G. Lafley, P&G's purpose is simple: "We create products and services that improve everyday life."

The second is company values or what is important to the organization. Dell is a company that recently went through a process of defining its values. According to CEO Kevin Rollins, "That led us to define the soul of Dell: focus on the customer, be open and direct in communications, be a good corporate citizen, have fun in winning."[2]

The third important part of vision is a long-term objective or what the organization wants to achieve over the long haul. This often takes the form of inspirational statement. For example, Teen Living Programs, a nonprofit organization dedicated to helping teens without a home in Chicago, has embraced this statement: "Teen Living Programs will be a model agency for the world, a shining example of a provider of services to youth who are homeless, recognized as a national leader in moving youth from homelessness to permanent independence."

Jim Collins and Jerry Porras refer to this as the envisioned future, the somewhat unreachable destination. "We recognize that the phrase *envisioned future* is somewhat paradoxical. On the one hand, it conveys concreteness—something visible, vivid, and real. On the other hand, it involves a time yet unrealized—with its dreams, hopes, and aspirations."[3]

Visions can take many forms; some are long and detailed, others are very simple. I recently visited a run-down barbecue restaurant near my office. There, taped to the wall on faded paper, was the following statement:

> *What We're About*
> Giving our customers the best BBQ anywhere
> Doing it with fun, flair, excellence, and excitement
> Serving our customers

A simple statement indeed, but one that captures what the organization is about; it conveys a sense of focus and values.

Simple or complex, basic or elegant, it is essential to have something that sets the long-term direction for a business, because a marketing plan always needs to be created with a sense of perspective.

STEP 3: CLARIFY THE GOALS AND OBJECTIVES

"We're going to restart this business!" proclaimed the dynamic new division general manager of a certain company. "We have harvested the business for too long. Starting today we are going to focus on innovation and growth!" The team cheered.

The team quickly got to work creating the innovation and growth plan. The plan included new products, improved quality, and a big investment in consumer marketing. Promotional spending and short-term sales incentives were cut.

Everything looked perfect, until one very small detail became apparent. Although the division manager believed passionately in growth and innovation, the CEO needed the division to continue delivering profits. The CEO believed, too, in growth and innovation, but not at the expense of short-term profitability.

When the division financial team actually started working on the numbers, it quickly became apparent that the innovation and growth plans were going to be very costly, and the only way to hit the targets set by the CEO was to ramp back the innovation and growth spending and focus on proven business-driving tactics, including promotional spending and short-term sales driving programs.

Therefore, gradually, the entire growth plan was taken apart, piece by piece. The general manager still proclaimed, "We will reinvigorate this business, focusing the right levers, not just the easy levers." But everyone knew that the truth was different; the growth plan had been shelved in favor of plan that would drive short-term profits.

The marketing plan had been built on mistaken profit expectations, which led to the entire plan being a huge waste of time.

A marketing plan that isn't built off a strong sense of objectives is asking for trouble. Indeed, you cannot create a strong marketing plan if you don't know the objectives for the business.

The third step in the marketing plan development process is clarifying the goals and objectives, understanding what the business needs to do over the course of the planning period, be that one, two, or three years.

This makes perfect sense. The entire reason for writing a marketing plan is to determine how best to achieve goals. As a result, clarifying the goals and objectives needs to come early in the planning process. Growing profit on a business by +50 percent, for example, requires a very different plan than growing profit by +2 percent. And there is little reason to start formulating a plan until you know which it is. Similarly, building brand equity requires a distinct set of initiatives; it is important to know whether that is a goal well before you get into creating a plan. As Conagra's Sergio Pereira advised, "... always start with the deliverables."

Confusion on goals can lead to a frustrating cycle, in which a team creates a marketing plan that achieves a certain set of numbers, but then is sent back to create a plan that delivers a different set of numbers. This inefficient spinning can be avoided by being clear on the goals upfront.

Managers should never *assume* they know what the goals are. This frequently leads to trouble. As John Gabarro and John Kotter wrote in their classic article, "Managing Your Boss," "The subordinate who passively assumes that he or she knows what the boss expects is in for trouble. Of course, some superiors will spell out their expectations very explicitly and in great detail. But most do not."[4]

Some argue that goals should be the *result* of the planning process, not the starting point, because a business can set appropriate goals only after completing the analysis, selecting the optimal strategic initiatives and tactics, and calculating the likely result. In other words, goals should be determined on the basis of a "bottom-up" analysis, not "top-down."

This makes logical sense but ignores the fact that for most businesses, the goals are not up for discussion. In general, there are clear targets that a business needs to deliver. In a public company, for example, investors have expectations for profit results. This means that the starting point for the marketing plan is clear: deliver the financial targets. When creating a marketing plan, a manager might as well start with the already established objectives. The objectives can be refined and clarified during the writing of the plan, but usually they're already floating around somewhere in the executive suite. As Adobe's Mark Delman observed, "Ultimately, for better or worse, shareholders have expectations, so the P&L has to drive." Marketing veteran Andy Whitman echoed the thought, stating, "The targets have to be upfront. If the company has given expectations to Wall Street, those are the expectations."

It is very rare that a "bottom-up" approach will ultimately deliver the needed profit number. For a variety of reasons, managers have a strong incentive to set very low targets. As a result, going through the process of rolling up financials is often a waste of time. For Conagra's Sergio Pereira, setting the objectives is a fundamental task of leadership: "Bottoms-up never gets you to your number. Bottoms-up is an abdication of responsibility."

Early in the process, the goals do not have to be set in stone. It doesn't really matter whether the profit target is +2, +2.5, or +3 percent; in all the cases the general goal is slow growth. Indeed, in some respects it is better if the goal is a bit loose; this provides more flexibility in the longer term. It does matter, however, if the goal is +2, +34, or +90 percent.

STEP 4: ANALYSIS, ANALYSIS, ANALYSIS

Once a team has checked the foundation and clarified the goals and objectives, it is time to get to the analysis. This is of course an essential step in the planning process; it impossible to create a good plan if you don't understand the business.

Ultimately, a business will succeed if it develops strategic initiatives that capitalize on the market trends and business strengths. This requires a deep understanding of the situation. As one marketing veteran observed, "Without a good sense of the market, I don't know how you create a marketing plan. I don't believe you can move forward without understanding what has been happening."

Analyzing the market is a working step; this phase is all about serious study and thinking. This step isn't about constructing presentation pages. The temptation to simply transfer data onto presentation pages is enormous, but this will ultimately lead to a very weak plan.

The analysis step is a risky one, though the risk in this step isn't that the ideas will be flawed or the analysis weak. The great risk is that team will get lost in the data and spend months wading through information that is interesting but not particularly useful. There is much to analyze on any business; it is not hard to fill the time with interesting contemplation and reflection. The problem is that simply analyzing data doesn't add a lot of value.

The analysis supporting a marketing plan should not focus on the business basics. The basics are probably well known, and in any event the business basics won't lead you to a new bold idea.

Instead, the analysis supporting a marketing plan should look at what is changing, and what is new. What are the changes in the market that might present opportunities or risks? What are the consumer trends that might create opportunities for growth? Where are the financial risks?

There are many ways to analyze a market, and there are many frameworks for a manager to apply. Many of these are very helpful. The key thing to remember, however, is that the focus should always be on what is new and what is changing and how that creates opportunities. Two basic analyses to consider are the SWOT analysis and the 3 Cs.

SWOT Analyses

No discussion of marketing plans would be complete without a review of the famous SWOT analysis. It is one of the most common and well-known analytical techniques available for understanding the situation facing a business.

A SWOT analysis is very simple. You take a paper and draw a two by two matrix. In one of the four boxes you list the strengths the business can build on (S), in the other boxes you list the weaknesses the business has to do deal with (W), the opportunities presenting themselves in the market (O), and the threats on the horizon (T). On one page you then have a summary of the situation facing a business.

Exhibit 5.1 SWOT Analysis Framework

Strengths	Opportunities
Weaknesses	Threats

The power of a SWOT analysis is that it forces you to consider each of these important topics. It provides an easy and usable framework for studying a business. Trying to figure out exactly what is happening on a business is challenging. Identifying the components of a SWOT analysis, however, is easy and straightforward.

A SWOT analysis is a useful tool, but like all tools it has limitations. One of the biggest issues is that it doesn't really lead anywhere. The analysis provides a good overview of the issues facing a business. However, it doesn't indicate what should be done. Connecting a SWOT analysis to strategic initiatives can be difficult.

3 Cs

Another very helpful framework for analyzing a business is the 3 Cs analysis. This analysis focuses on understanding a business's customers, competitors, and channel partners. Analyzing each of these players is critical to understand the situation facing a business.

Just like a SWOT analysis, the 3 Cs provides a simple and clear starting point for analysis. Unfortunately, just like a SWOT, the analysis doesn't lead logically to action; it is simply a solid and useful approach to build a deeper understanding of the business.

Customers are the people who ultimately buy and use your product or service. These are the people who matter most. Understanding the issues they face, their concerns, and their needs is a basic marketing step. It is impossible to succeed if you don't understand and delight your customers.

Competitors also play a critical role in market planning; anything a company attempts to do will be affected by the actions of competitors. Competitors are an unfortunate fact of life in the world of business; life would be much easier without them. In many ways, competition is the most challenging factor for business leaders; if there were no competition, business success would be fairly assured. Indeed, as Conagra's Sergio Pereira observed, "Strategy is ultimately a competitive game."

Weak competitive analysis is a problem in many plans; the team comes up with a host of interesting strategies and tactics, but it neglects to consider the competition. Tropicana's John Bauer has seen the importance of competitive analysis. He stated, "Most marketers do not really understand how they stack up to competitors. They don't spend enough time understanding the competition."

Channel issues are important and frequently neglected. If a business doesn't form strong relationships with channel partners such as retailers and distributors, it can be blocked from the market entirely. If your customers don't have access to a product because your channel partners don't carry it, your customers can't and won't buy.

The 3 Cs analysis is a useful way to analyze the changes facing a business, as well as the opportunities. Successful marketing plans are built on a deep understanding of all three.

STEP 5: IDENTIFY STRATEGIC INITIATIVES AND TACTICS

Step 5, identifying strategic initiatives and tactics, is the most important step in the planning process. This is the step that actually drives the value of the plan; in many ways the first four steps all build to this step.

This is also the most difficult part of the planning process, because it entails narrowing your options. Given all the things you can do on the business, what will you focus on?

Most businesses have dozens of potential strategic initiatives, and these initiatives almost always appear to be very attractive. The challenge in this step of the planning process is to find the most compelling strategic initiatives to pursue and the best tactics to use to achieve each one.

This is hard work; the options are numerous, and making decisions can be difficult. Human nature will encourage you to have many options, each one very broad, giving you the freedom to do almost anything. This is not an effective approach.

The question is really quite simple: what needs to happen to drive growth? Big picture, where will the growth come from?

Developing strategic initiatives is not easy. Sifting through reams of data, forming judgments about future trends, and then selecting the three or four best initiatives can be incredibly challenging. Starwood's Barry Sternlicht has observed that some people struggle with identifying strategies for a business. He explained, "Even with all the facts in front of them . . . some brilliant people still can't form good opinions because they can't figure out what the data in front of them means."[5]

Three Questions

When thinking about strategic initiatives, it is useful to ask three simple questions about a business. These questions can help define the opportunities on a business and narrow down the focal points.

Question 1: Grow Share or Grow the Category?
The sales of any business are a function of the size of the overall industry, or the category, and the market share of the company. Indeed, the following formula is always true:

$$\text{Category Sales} \times \text{Product Market Share} = \text{Product Sales}$$

The size of the category times the market share for a particular product will always equal the sales of the product. This is analytically true. If a category has unit sales of 2 million units for example, and a particular business has a unit market share of 25 percent, then the sales of that business will be 500,000 units. Category times share will always equal sales.

As a result, if sales are going to go up, either share or category will have to increase in size. If the category is flat, and market share is flat, then sales will be flat. This is analytically true 100 percent of the time.

A marketer can then ask a rather simple question: What is more important, increasing the size of the category or increasing our market share?

This may seem like a rather abstract question, but it is actually critically important, because the tactics to build the category are very different from the tactics to increase market share. For example, financial services giant UBS could increase sales in its personal financial services business by building the overall category; it could tell people that having a professionally developed financial plan is important, and it could highlight the tax benefits of establishing a trust. However, UBS could also focus on building share; in this case, UBS might explain what makes UBS particularly good versus other financial services companies, or it might provide a discount to lure competitors' customers.

It is very difficult to build category and share at the same time, because the tactics are very different. Initiatives that build the category are all about increasing the size of the industry. Initiatives that increase share focus on building differentiation versus other competitors. An initiative that builds the category will generally do little to build share, and an initiative that builds share will do little to build the category. A manager has to choose.

Question 2: Penetration or Buying Rate?

Sales on a business are always a function of how many customers the business has and how frequently they purchase. This, mathematically, must always be true.

Penetration measures the number of customers. Buying rate is the average number of purchases over a period of time, frequently one year. So the following formula is always true:

$$\text{Penetration} \times \text{Buying Rate} = \text{Sales}$$

The number of customers (penetration) times the average rate of purchase among the customers (buying rate) will always equal sales.

The only way sales on a business will increase is if either penetration is going up, or buying rate is going up. If the number of customers remains constant (penetration) and the rate at which they purchase doesn't change (buying rate) then sales will not change.

So a manager should think about another very simple question: What is more important, increasing penetration or increasing buying rate?

As with growing category and increasing share, the tactics for increasing penetration are very different from the tactics for increasing buying rate. To increase penetration, a business has to go out and find new customers. This process will often involve broad marketing efforts, with some very high-value incentives to get people in the door. To build buying rate, a business has to get current users buying more. This will frequently involve targeted marketing efforts, with incentives that reward loyalty or size of purchase.

A coupon in the Sunday newspaper is a marketing tactic that could be used to support growth in penetration or buying rate. But it would be very different depending on what it was trying to achieve. To build penetration, the headline might say "Try This Great Tasting Product!," and the coupon might be a high-value offer off of one item. To build penetration, the headline might communicate a usage idea, such as "Try This New Recipe!" and the coupon would probably offer a low value offer for a multiple purchase.

As a result, thinking about penetration and buying rate is important.

Question 3: Awareness, Trial, or Repeat?
For any product to be adopted by a customer, three things must occur. First, the customer has to be made aware of the product. At a very basic level, the customer has to know the product exists. Second, the customer has to try it. Nothing will happen unless a customer actually tries the product. Third, the customer has to come back after the trial experience and buy the product again. In other words, they have to repeat on the product.

This progression is true for any product in the world; the steps are the same everywhere.

$$\text{Awareness} \quad \rightarrow \quad \text{Trial} \quad \rightarrow \quad \text{Repeat}$$

So the third question to consider when creating strategic initiatives is this: What is more important, awareness, trial, or repeat?

As with the other questions, the tactics for each of these things are different. Tactics that build awareness are different from tactics that build trial, and these are different from tactics that build repeat. It is impossible to do everything at the same time.

Being clear on the challenge is essential. If you don't know whether awareness is more important than repeat or less important, it will be impossible to formulate a plan; the tactics that do one thing very well usually do another thing very poorly. A piece of mass-market advertising, for example, is likely to be good at building awareness, but not effective at all at building repeat. A coupon printed on the inside of a package is a terrible awareness building tactic but is probably quite effective for repeat.

Profit Equation

The goal of any for profit business is to make money, and this is an important matter for many nonprofit ventures as well. When all is said and done, profit needs to go up. This is why profit is so often one of the goals in marketing plans. Profit is what matters most.

It is useful, then, to understand some basic finance. You don't need to know much about hedge funds and derivatives to create a marketing plan, but you do have to know a bit about finance and the way a business makes money.

On a very simple level, the pre-tax profit of any company is simply the sum of profit from one business unit, plus the profit from the next business unit, plus the profit from the next business unit, less corporate overhead less the cost of capital.

$$\text{Company Profit} = (\text{Profit from business } 1 + \text{Profit from business } 2) - \text{Overhead} - \text{Cost of Capital}$$

So at Microsoft, for example, the company's profit is the profit from Windows plus the profit from Office minus the losses on every other business unit less corporate overhead such as Bill's salary and the company jet.

The profit on a particular business is always a function of the amount of units the business sells, times the margin made on each unit, less the marketing expense involved to achieve those sales, less the direct overhead. In an equation, it looks like this:

$$\text{Business Profit} = (\text{Units x Margin}) - \text{Marketing Expense} - \text{Overhead}$$

As discussed earlier, unit sales on a business are always a function of the size of the market (category) times the portion of the market that goes to that company (share). Margin is always price less cost of goods sold (COGS). Marketing expense includes things such as advertising, promotions, and public relations efforts. Overhead includes the cost of the office space, R&D expense, salaries, benefits, and other things.

Combined, then, you get an equation that summarizes in a very simple way the profitability of virtually any business.

P = Business Unit Profit
C = Size of the Category
S = Market Share
OH = Overhead Expenses
M = Marketing Expense

$$P = ((C \times S) \times (\text{Price} - \text{COGS})) - M - OH$$

This equation is a useful tool for thinking about a business. If profit is going up, something in the equation must be working in favor of the business. The category must be growing, or market share must be increasing, or pricing must be going up or some other factor must be working. There isn't anything else.

It is possible to analyze most businesses using this equation; by thinking through the parts you can get a good understanding of the challenges facing the business. By looking at the trends affecting each part of the equation, it is fairly easy to see the profit picture.

The Gillette razor business is a good example of this. In the United States, the category trend is basically flat; the population is growing slowly and most people shave. Gillette has a very high market share, and the market share is basically flat. The only brands left in the market of note are Schick, Bic, and store brands. Share isn't likely to go up much going forward. Cost of goods sold is small (plastic and metal) and probably flat; the cost of producing a razor is not substantial. Marketing expenses and overhead are both probably flat. The only lever that is increasing for Gillette is price, and this will remain the key lever going forward. To grow profits, Gillette has to find a way to steadily increase prices. Historically, Gillette has done this by launching new products, each one more expensive than the last. Many years ago Gillette launched Trac Two. Later the company introduced Atra, then Sensor, then Sensor Excel, then Mach 3, then Mach 3 Turbo, then Mach 3 Power, then, most recently, Fusion. Will Gillette continue with this approach going forward? Given the profit equation and the importance of price, it is highly likely that there will be more new products in the future.

The profit equation is a wonderful tool for identifying strategic initiatives. When looking at the equation, it is useful to study each lever. Is reducing cost a big opportunity? Is building share? Is growing the category? Each of these questions can lead to a strategic initiative.

Remember, though, that a business can't do everything at the same time. It is impossible to grow the category, increase market share, raise prices, cut costs, optimize marketing spending, and reduce overhead all at the same time. Once again, you have to choose.

Initiatives to Tactics

Once the strategic initiatives are clear, then it is possible to look at the tactics. Tactics are the specific programs and activities that will ensure the success of the strategic initiative. Importantly, it is impossible to select tactics until the strategic initiatives are clear. Every tactic should be linked to an initiative.

The process, then, is to first identify the big initiatives and then think about tactics, or how the initiative will come to pass. The first step should always be identifying the initiatives; the second step should always be tactics.

Developing great tactics requires analytical rigor. You have to know the numbers behind the tactics to get a sense for what will work. This is where return on investment (ROI) should come up as a discussion point; what is the most efficient way to execute against the strategic initiative?

Great tactics also require creativity. Some of the best marketing programs are the most unexpected, simply because these tactics attract attention and generate excitement.

The challenge when formulating tactics is to think broadly about different ideas, and then use analytical rigor to select the most compelling options.

STEP 6: CHECK THE NUMBERS

By this point in the planning process, much of the plan is complete; the goals are set, the strategic initiatives are clear, and the tactics are penciled in. Things seem relatively complete.

The next step, however, is also critically important. Before going any further, it is essential to check the numbers and look at the overall financial picture to be sure the plan holds together and the numbers work. This involves creating a rough profit and loss (P&L) statement for the business, including rough estimates of sales, revenue, spending, and profitability.

This is a critical stage in the process; a marketing plan will only work if the numbers actually hold together. When the plan is quantified, the profits have to be achievable.

In many cases, this is where things become difficult. For most people, identifying things to do isn't all that hard; there are all sorts of good tactics to pursue. Making sure the figures all hold together is much harder. As Adobe's Mark Delman observed, "It's one thing to say you want to grow 10 percent a year. It's another to really understand how you will get there."

Importantly, the focus should be on developing a rough P&L that uses *reasonable* assumptions. Attempting to finalize every aspect of the financials is not a productive exercise; it requires too much time, and the financials take over the plan. Detailed financials should be created as part of the annual budgeting process, not the marketing planning process.

The key question in this section is whether the recommended initiatives and tactics will deliver the financial objectives. Will the plan succeed? If it's clear that the plan won't deliver the profit goal, then the team must rethink the plan. It may be that the strategic initiatives are not appropriate given the financial expectations, or that the tactics are too costly. If the financials don't work, the team should go back several steps to complete more analysis and review the strategic initiatives and tactics.

Pushing forward with a marketing plan when it is clear that the financials don't work is a mistake; the plan will ultimately be doomed. Either the business will miss the projections, which is an unpleasant proposition, or it will need to take additional steps to achieve the projections, in which case the team should have made these critical decisions during the planning process. As Dave Barger, CEO of JetBlue Airways observed, "Hope isn't a plan. You better assume that plan B is not going to materialize, either, so what's plan C and D?"[6]

In some cases, achieving the financial projections for a business requires drastic and strategically foolish actions; the business might have to cut all its equity spending, or reduce product quality so much that it jeopardizes the customer satisfaction, or take a price increase that will generate profit in the short term but create problems in the long term.

In this situation, the team should review the issue with senior management before creating a full marketing plan to determine the best course of action. Ideally, targets can come down to allow for a feasible plan. Worst case, if extreme action is necessary, then everyone understands that the plan will damage the business.

Step 7: Sell the Plan

Before a marketing plan can be implemented, it needs support from senior executives in the company and from cross-functional groups. A brilliant plan that lacks the support of the organization is essentially useless; the plan will never be executed. Similarly, the best strategic initiatives will do nothing if key cross-functional players don't support them; the initiatives will not get implemented. As a result, selling the plan is a critical step.

This step includes writing the actual marketing plan and presenting it to key people, and then securing approval and support.

Importantly, this step should only commence after all the preceding steps are finished; before the writing begins, the team must complete the analysis, develop the strategies and tactics, and check the financials. Indeed, starting to write a plan before the strategic initiatives and tactics are clear often leads to weak plans, full of pages that contain accurate data but say nothing.

The process of writing and communicating a plan is not easy, and it is not quick. This step takes significant time. All too often teams spend so much time creating the plan and checking the numbers that they neglect to set aside enough time to do a good job writing the plan down. This, of course, is an enormous mistake. At the end of the day, the plan must be written; shortchanging this part of the process is an easy way to get into trouble.

When writing a marketing plan, the goal is to lay out the recommended goals and objectives, strategic initiatives, and tactics (GOST), and then explain precisely why they will work.

The plan then has to be presented to key decision makers, both senior executives and cross-functional leaders. Gaining true support is essential; the goal is to ensure that people truly believe in the ideas. Tepid support is a particularly dangerous thing; the team walks away thinking the plan is a go, but later discovers that many questions remain. This is frustrating and dysfunctional. As Gary Ramey, senior vice president at Gold Toe Brands observed, "You have to get everybody together. If everybody doesn't buy in, you have confusion."

Early in my career, a colleague advised me to be wary of, as he called them, "the grinners." These are people who will grin in a meeting, and say very pleasant things, but later disagree with the recommendations. He was right, of course. "The grinners" seem positive, but can be extremely destructive. If you encounter some of these people, it is best to spend extra time meeting with them, to be sure you know where they stand and can address their issues.

Once senior management signs on to the plan, it is essential to then communicate it to the extended business team. This includes all the people who work on a business regularly. People have to know what the plan is to feel a part of the business, and any leader wants her team to be fired up and engaged. The best way to do this is to be certain the team understands the plan and believes it will happen. This is particularly important at larger organizations. As Allen Questrom, CEO of J.C. Penney, explains, "The bigger the company, the more you have to sell the strategy to the organization. The more people who understand the strategy, the more likely it will get executed."[7]

The process of communicating with the extended team includes meeting to go through the plan, answering questions, and conveying excitement and enthusiasm. It involves telling people about the plan in multiple venues, including e-mail messages, business update meetings, and individual meetings.

There are two essential things to keep in mind when communicating with the larger team. First, it is best to do this only once the plan has been approved by senior management. Taking the team through a bold plan that eventually is not approved can do terrible things for morale. There is little reason to get people fired up about a set of strategic initiatives and exciting tactics until you are confident the plan will actually come to fruition.

At one point in my career I was leading a team responsible for a small but promising brand. The team was passionate about the brand, and truly believed the brand could grow into a much larger business. So, working with the team, I created a plan to jump-start the business with new products and new advertising. I then took the entire team through the complete plan. It was an impressive piece of work, and the team was excited about the potential of actually building the brand they loved so much.

Unfortunately, I wasn't able to sell the plan to senior management. There was an element of risk in the plan; it was not certain that the new products would work and that the advertising would have the intended impact. And, when all was said and done, I couldn't convince the division general manager to take a risk on a small business; he was willing to take risks, but he had to be selective about it, and other brands were taking some big risks at the same time.

The unfortunate result was that my team was discouraged. The bold, exciting plan wasn't going to happen. Instead, the challenge was to prop things up and build profits with a set of small, tactical moves. This was not an inspiring picture.

The learning is that there is a time to tell the extended team about the marketing plan, and it is essential to do this. But the time is not until you are confident that the plan is actually going to happen.

The other thing to keep in mind when communicating with the larger team is that the message should be positive. There are two ways to look at any plan. There is the pragmatic, somewhat cynical look that savvy, experienced executives often provide, with a focus on looking for the holes and the risks and the uncertainties. There is also the upbeat, positive, and excited look, with a focus on the big ideas and the potential.

When communicating a marketing plan to the broader team, it is best to take the upbeat, positive view; there is no reason to explain to the entire team why the plan might not work, and why the plan isn't really attainable, and why everything might collapse.

The goal when communicating with the team is to build understanding, commitment, and enthusiasm.

Step 8: Execute and Track Progress

A marketing plan is completely useless until it is executed. The best ideas written on paper will do nothing to build profits and sales until they are brought to life in the market. Execution is critical. As P&G's A.G Lafley observed, "The only strategy anyone ever sees is what is executed in the market."

There is a long-standing debate in the business world about the importance of strategy and execution. Some people argue that strategy is most important, because a bad strategy will fail regardless of the execution. If you execute a terrible strategy brilliantly well, according to this argument, you will simply fail faster and in a bigger way. Other people argue that execution is most important, because the best strategy in the world will fail if the execution is weak. A wonderful new product won't sell if the product doesn't ever get on to the shelf, or if the product isn't in stock when people want to try it. The truth is, obviously enough, that both matter. Strategy is important and execution is important. You need both.

A good marketing plan leads to good execution; people know what to do, senior management provides the needed resources, and the core direction is clear. This is how a great marketing plan drives a business; when all is said and done, a business with a strong plan has direction and focus, which leads to positive long-term results for the organization.

There are many factors that drive strong execution. Indeed, the topic of execution could fill a large book, and it has, many times over. There is far too much to explore in depth here.

However, two things are particularly important when it comes to linking marketing plans to execution. First, the next steps should be clear. For the plan to proceed, a marketing plan has to identify what needs to happen and when. Without some clear next steps, there is a great risk that the plan will simply be filed away and ignored.

Second, there needs to be milestones to evaluate how well things are going. Ideally, each strategic initiative should have a set of metrics, which give an indication of whether or not the initiative is coming to pass.

If a strategic initiative is building awareness on a new product, for example, it would be reasonable to have specific awareness goals. By the end of the first quarter, awareness should be at 25 percent, and by the end of the second quarter awareness should be at 50 percent. If awareness is only at 15 percent at the end of the first quarter, then clearly something needs to be done to adjust course.

A good marketing plan makes it easy to manage the business. If the key milestones are clear, a leader can watch them to be sure things are proceeding and the business is on track. At business update meetings, the team can focus on four simple questions:

> Where are we on implementation of the marketing plan?
> How well is it working?
> Has anything significant changed since the plan was created?
> If so, what should we do now?

These four questions can drive implementation and execution for the team, and ensure that the plan is actually coming to fruition.

AROUND AND AROUND

In the ideal world, the marketing plan development process flows step by step in a sequential fashion. One step leads to the next, and this in turn leads to execution of the plan and strong business results. Therefore, the planning process is linear, orderly, and direct.

Exhibit 5.2   Linear Marketing Plan Development Process

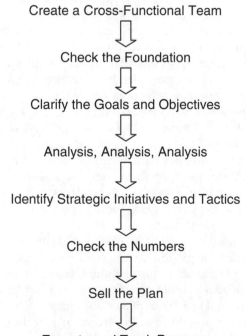

Create a Cross-Functional Team

⇩

Check the Foundation

⇩

Clarify the Goals and Objectives

⇩

Analysis, Analysis, Analysis

⇩

Identify Strategic Initiatives and Tactics

⇩

Check the Numbers

⇩

Sell the Plan

⇩

Execute and Track Progress

However, seeing marketing planning as a nice linear process, with a clear start and a clear finish, is actually a bit misleading. Things are not quite this neat and simple. There are two reasons for this.

First, when creating a marketing plan, you may have to go back a step at certain times in the process. If you have trouble identifying strategic initiatives, for example, you will need to go back to the analysis step. If you find the financials don't work, you may need to circle back to the objectives, to set a more achievable set of targets, or to analysis, to look afresh at the data and find other opportunities.

Very frequently, when trying to sell the plan you will discover things don't hold together. It might be that the plan doesn't seem to flow, or the analysis seems insufficient to support your case, or senior management doesn't agree with your point of view. In any of these cases, you need to step back, perhaps to think more about the strategic initiatives and tactics, perhaps to do more analysis, perhaps to check the foundation once again.

Creating a plan can be a frustrating undertaking in this respect; there are some days when you think you are moving forward but in reality you are moving back. Indeed, going back to do more analysis after you thought the plan was done can be discouraging. However, plans improve dramatically through this process; if there are holes in the plan, and there often are, it is better to find them and address them before the plan is executed.

Second, creating a marketing plan is not a one-time event; it is not a static process. The planning process doesn't stop when execution begins. As soon as the plan is set and the team begins carrying out the tactics, it's time to begin working on the next iteration of the plan, and the process begins again. As AspireUp's Roland Jacobs observed, "The planning cycle is a continuous loop."

If life were static, a business could develop a marketing plan and then rely on it for several years, at least until the strategies were all achieved and the tactics were brought to fruition. Unfortunately, that's not reality; life is constantly changing and evolving. As a result, marketing plans are iterative documents; a business leader may revise marketing plans many times a year as situations change.

This is what keeps things challenging. Nestlé's Steven Cunliffe stated, "Life never entirely goes as it is planned. There are always changes, and you have to adapt to them."

Any time the situation facing a business changes substantially, the marketing plan should be reviewed, because what was a good idea one day may no longer be a good idea the following day. If a competitor launches a major new product, for example, the marketing plan may need to focus on defense. If product costs shoot up, pricing may become incredibly important, or cost reductions may suddenly become essential.

It is conceivable that a business team will need to create many marketing plans in a single year, each one modified based on the latest situation. Indeed, in a fast-moving industry marketing plans will need to be updated

Exhibit 5.3   Marketing Plan Development Process

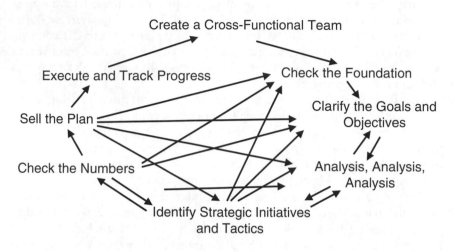

and refined constantly. As Unilever's Andrew Gross noted, "As soon as you put together the document it is out of date."

And indeed, the simple concept that life is always changing is perhaps one of the most forceful arguments in favor of creating simple, focused marketing plans. It is impossible to update a 200-page plan frequently. It is very possible to update a 15-page plan.

In reality, marketing planning is a process that never really ends.

*   *   *

It would be nice if you could simply sit down and, in a few hours, develop a marketing plan that would lead to guaranteed great results. Unfortunately, this is not the way things go. The best way to create a strong plan is to set aside enough time so that you can follow the important steps. Each step in the process plays an essential role, and skipping any of them can lead to trouble.

CHAPTER 6

Writing the Plan

After all the analysis, discussion, and brainstorming, someone has to actually write a marketing plan. It doesn't just appear. Putting a marketing plan down on a paper is a critical step in the process. This step includes a bit of writing, a bit of strategy, a bit of analytical thinking, and a bit of showmanship. This is the place where everything comes together. It is in many ways the most important part of the process.

A marketing plan has to be written—and written well—to have an impact. A marketing plan that never gets written down will rarely succeed. Similarly, a plan that is written in an incoherent fashion won't generally work. This is true for three reasons.

First, until a plan is actually written down, it is simply a collection of ideas. Through the writing process, the plan takes shape and becomes real. Writing a plan down on paper forces commitment and clarity; it forces a manager to be precise on the recommendation. It is one thing to emphatically declare, "We need to invest in our brands and increase innovation!" Or, "We should invest in advertising and public relations, and reduce spending on promotions." It is a very different thing to write down precisely what this entails and how the ideas fit into the overall plan. Investing in advertising and reducing promotions are lovely ideas, of course, but until the overall plan is created the ideas are just that: ideas.

Second, and perhaps more important, the people who will see the plan only see the final document. They don't see the interim steps. They don't see the process. They don't see the discussions, the analysis, or the debate. They only see the written plan; they see the recommendations, the logic, and the facts.

The people reviewing a plan really don't care about the work that went into creating it. The fact that a team spent weeks analyzing a market, or devoted three full days to debating alternatives, or constructed an elaborate multivariate regression to forecast the market size, is completely irrelevant to the merits of the plan. Dutifully following the steps of a marketing planning process is good, but it is not a substitute for a strong recommendation. A team that carefully follows a process and produces a muddled marketing plan has achieved very little indeed.

The people reviewing a marketing plan simply see the plan. The written document is the output. This is true whether a plan is fully written out, or simply a presentation. If the plan is well assembled and well crafted, it will make sense and generally be approved. If it is hard to follow, the plan will be challenged, questioned, and debated—and rightly so. This is true for senior executives, the people who will ultimately approve the plan. It is also true for the team that will execute the plan. In both cases, the written document has to hold together: it has to be credible, and it has to be convincing.

Third, writing a plan is a valuable process because issues frequently appear only as the plan takes shape on paper. One marketing veteran observed, "... people don't REALLY make decisions until the information must get put down on paper. The process of writing the plan actually becomes the process of forcing and finalizing all the important decisions. No one makes a real decision until something's written down on paper and the decision is in danger of being disseminated widely by a certain deadline."

Major issues have a rather unfortunate way of surfacing as the plan is being written, when the excitement of the brainstorming session has dissipated and all that is left is the plan on a page. Ideas that seemed wonderful in the moment frequently seem questionable when written down on a piece of paper, much as a piece of art purchased on a tropical vacation sometimes seems out of place and amateurish when unwrapped at home.

The fact that there really is no money to fund innovation often comes up only when all the priorities are identified, and the cost of all the planned programs far exceeds the available money. The fact that a competitor is probably going to react to a sharp increase in promotion spending with a similar increase, thereby negating the volume impact, sometimes becomes clear only when the rationale for the increase is written down.

Obvious questions tend to come up when a plan is put down on paper. Won't competitors react? Didn't we try that last year? Where will we get the money? Will consumers really respond to that? Is that enough advertising to break through?

As a result, writing a great plan is essential. A manager must actually create a document that communicates, persuades, resonates, and inspires.

The writing phase is where many marketing plans go off the track; the ideas might be solid, but the plan never takes shape on paper. Somehow the concepts get muddled when written down. This is a big issue. If the ideas are great but the actual written plan is disjointed, the overall impact of the entire planning process will be nil; the great ideas will be lost in the muddle of the plan.

For many people, writing can be a struggle. Most business executives spend their days running from a meeting to a presentation to the airport and then to another meeting, checking voicemails and messages while on the fly. The day is full of stimulation, demands, and action. It is hard to then carve out a big block of time, sit down, and write a plan.

This is why many marketing executives delay and delay the writing process far too long. When faced with the prospect of working on writing a marketing plan, they look, desperately, for other things to do: check e-mails, return phone calls, organize the desk, and go through the change drawer. As one of my colleagues explained, "I would rather pick up dog poop with my hand than sit down to write something."

Writing a marketing plan is particularly difficult, because by the time the writing process starts, the team is often frazzled, exhausted both mentally and physically from the analysis and plan development. Writing the plan is frequently not a step anyone looks forward to.

However, procrastination is a dangerous thing when it comes to creating a marketing plan, because marketing plans get much better when they're actually written down. In addition, the process of writing can take a long time, with multiple drafts and versions. Delaying simply reduces the time for refinement and improvement.

All too often the writing phase is left for the very end of the plan development process, when time is short and energy flagging. Only when the deadline approaches does anyone sit down to write the plan. This is not a wise approach; marketing plans don't write themselves, and good plans take time, energy, and effort.

But Wait

All the above being said, you must very carefully pick the time in the process when you begin writing the plan. Start too early and you won't be solid on the proposals. Start too late and you won't have time to flesh out problems that might pop up during the writing process.

When it comes to writing a marketing plan, you can't start actually writing a marketing plan until you're clear on the plan. You have to know what you are recommending before you can write a recommendation. You have to know the goals and objectives, the strategic initiatives, and the tactics (GOST). Indeed, if you can't complete the GOST framework chart, you're not ready to write the plan. The classic admonition, "Never put off until tomorrow what you can do today" simply does not apply when it comes to marketing plans. You have to wait until you know the basic recommendation before you can start writing a plan.

Some particularly energetic people will be tempted to start writing plan early in the plan development process, because it gives the impression of progress. If the goal is to create a written plan, the logic goes, then actually writing something seems like a good thing to do. After all, progress is progress. In addition, as the word count increases and the pages multiply, it appears that the marketing plan is actually taking shape. This is encouraging for everyone involved.

Unfortunately, writing a marketing plan before you know the recommendation is a bad idea, because it is almost impossible to do. The document might look substantial. However, this would simply be an illusion, much like a Hollywood movie set in which buildings look substantial but are just fronts with nothing behind.

In many respects, writing without a recommendation does far more harm than good, because in the absence of a recommendation, all you can write down is facts, analysis, and learning. This seems fine, but this material adds nothing on its own; it needs to be connected to the overall story.

Starting the writing process too early is actually one main reason that marketing plans become so bloated. Once pages exist, they tend to stay, filling up a plan with useless, distracting information. Studies into human behavior consistently show that people hate to give things up. Once people have something, they want to keep it. This is true, too, with material in a presentation; people hate to discard pages. This is one reason why so many marketing plans end up as long, convoluted documents that people ignore.

The other problem with writing a plan before the recommendation is clear is that it can distract you from the real task of figuring out what should be done. Laying out data is fairly easy. It is also, in a strange way, satisfying; it gives the impression of productivity. Identifying strategic initiatives and tactics and making sure the plan holds together is hard. As a result, people can lose focus on the bigger issues.

While at Kraft Foods, I had the opportunity to manage a number of summer interns. Each had a project they worked on during the summer. For example, an intern on Kraft BBQ sauce might look at opportunities to market to Hispanic consumers, and an intern on A.1. steak sauce might try to determine whether the brand should partner with meat packers. Each intern gave a presentation at the end of the 10-week internship. The presentation played an important role in determining whether the intern would receive a coveted offer to join the company as a full-time employee.

I quickly learned that without clear guidance, interns would fall into an obvious and dangerous trap: they would get lost in the data and then lost in the writing process. At the start of the summer, an intern would look around for relevant information and would discover, in almost every case, a virtually unlimited trove of data and facts. Then the intern would start gathering up this information, making copies, and printing documents. After six or seven weeks of this, the intern would find himself with a huge stack of data and no recommendations. This would lead to a sense of panic, so the intern would start creating a presentation, producing page after page. With a few days left in the summer, the intern would then discover that he or she had a long, impressive collection of pages with absolutely no ideas and no recommendations. The final days would be a terrible, sleepless scramble in a desperate bid to salvage something of interest from the mass of data.

Before starting to write a marketing plan, then, it is essential to be clear on the recommendation. What precisely is the plan? If the answer isn't clear, it isn't time to start writing; it is time to keep working on the core plan.

This is not to say that the plan has to be 100 percent locked before the writing process starts. Indeed, very often gaps in the plan become apparent as the writing goes on; this forces the team to go back to an earlier step in the process and results in a better finished product. It is wise to leave time for this. Still, you can't start writing until you know the basic message.

Getting the recommendations fully agreed upon and finalized by the business team can be a tough job. It is wise to use a deadline force the issue with the team; decisions sometimes only get made when they must finally be committed to paper.

Who's Your Audience?

Before you can write a strong marketing plan, it is essential to think about your audience. Indeed, every marketing plan should be written with a specific person in mind. Sometimes a plan will be given to a group of people, but even in this case there is generally one key decision maker to focus on.

Thinking about your audience is important, because the better you know your audience, the more likely you can create a recommendation that will resonate. Just as it's foolish to start working on an advertising campaign until you know your target market very well, so too is it foolish to start writing a marketing plan until you know who will be reviewing it.

The goal for a manager isn't simply to survive the marketing plan presentation, though this is how some people seem to view the process. The goal is to get strong, committed support. If the presentation is to a senior executive, the goal is endorsement and resources. If the presentation is to a cross-functional team, the goal is enthusiasm and commitment.

To get support, you must think about your audience and write your plan in a way that will resonate and motivate. There are a number of important questions to answer about your audience before starting to write the plan.

What Is Their Style?

This is a very basic question. Does your audience like to read plans or listen to presentations? Most people have a preference. As legendary business strategist Peter Drucker observed, "Far too few people even know that there are readers and listeners and that people are rarely both."[1]

Giving a long, detailed, written plan to a person who likes presentations will not work particularly well; they may well not read the plan at all. Similarly, giving a presentation to a person who likes to read and think about material isn't going to work, either; they may long for more information and detail, and they need time to think about and process the plan.

Understanding whether your audience is a reader or listener has some immediate practical implications, because marketing plans can be written documents or presented documents, and the preference of the audience should drive the decision. More important, the amount of information and the amount of commentary will be driven by the format. If you are presenting, you don't need to include every nuance and piece of the story; you can speak to these details in the presentation. If you're submitting a document, however, the written word is all you have, so you must pay close attention to the writing and include all the key facts in the written document.

In organizations that have a clear marketing plan process, it will often be readily apparent whether the plan should be a written document or a presentation. Nonetheless, it is still important to know the preferences of your audience; if you are creating a presentation for someone who likes to read, for example, you will have more robust pages with more information. If the presentation is for someone who likes to listen, the presentation should have less information and rely heavily on the spoken word.

What Do They Know?

You must consider how much the audience knows about the business before writing the plan. If your audience is very familiar with the business, you can move quickly to the recommendations, building on what they already know. If your audience has limited knowledge of the business, however, you will need more explanation.

People have to know a business fairly well to understand the marketing plan. For example, it is impossible to assess a marketing plan for the Blue Bonnet brand of margarine if you don't know that Blue Bonnet is a brand of mainstream margarine, which is an intensely competitive market with many fine but relatively undifferentiated brands battling for share largely on the basis on price, and that price is largely driven by product cost, which is in turn driven by the rather volatile soybean oil commodity market.

If you are presenting a plan to someone who has very little knowledge of a particular business, you should seriously consider holding a separate meeting before the marketing plan presentation to provide an overview of the category and the industry and cover the basics of the business. Understanding the industry is critical for appreciating the marketing plan, but attempting to both introduce an industry and present a marketing plan at same time makes no sense at all; it is simply too much material for people to absorb in one long meeting.

Indeed, one of the reasons marketing plans often end up as long, cumbersome documents is that people feel the need to review basic industry details while presenting the plan. This can't be done, or at least it can't be done well; one part or the other will inevitably suffer.

What Are They Worried About?

The focus of marketing is meeting customer needs. The most important and fundamental marketing lesson is that people don't buy things just because they are good quality and fairly priced. People buy things that meet a need. As a result, a basic marketing task is thinking about the needs of your customer; what is my customer interested in? What is my customer worried about? What are my customer's needs?

Executives should think about marketing plans in a similar manner; the plan is the product, the decision maker is the customer. A critical question, then, is: What are my customer's needs? More important, perhaps is this question: What is my customer worried about? How will my product meet my customer's needs and address my customer's worries? The simple truth is this: a plan that responds to and meets the needs of the customer will be more likely to be well received than a plan that doesn't.

For example, if you are presenting to the CEO and you know that she is feeling enormous pressure from the board of directors and impatient investors to deliver good financial results, then the marketing plan needs to clearly address short-term profits. This is not the time for a plan that focuses on the long-term potential of the brand. The issue on the table is short-term profitability. Similarly, if you are presenting to someone who believes in the power of innovation and growth, the plan should of course highlight innovation and growth.

Importantly, the goal isn't to just present what your audience wants to hear. Some people attempt to do this, as if the entire marketing plan process is something of a game, where the manager attempts to figure out what the senior executive wants to hear and then says exactly that. This is a rather tempting approach, because it is easy and popular. If you know a senior executive wants to increase prices on a business, for example, then including a price increase in the plan will help the plan presentation go smoothly. Similarly, if you know there is an interest in new products, then recommending new products seems like a logical approach. Moreover, recommending a change in advertising agencies will be viewed as a good idea by someone who wants to change advertising agencies.

However, simply presenting what you think a senior executive wants to hear is a bad approach. Most important, this is an abrogation of the duties of leadership; it turns the marketing plan into an elaborate ritual of "corporate-think." It is no fun to present ideas that you don't believe in, and this approach is not likely to be successful. It is the rare executive who can present a plan with conviction when they don't actually believe in it. And, at the end of the day, the person presenting the plan is usually accountable for delivering it.

The goal is to present the recommendations that are right for the business in a way that will maximize the odds that your recommendations will be approved. In this context, understanding the perspective of your audience is essential; it helps you communicate clearly and then position your ideas in a positive light.

What Are They Thinking?

Presenting a plan that is likely to be well received is very different than presenting a plan that will be poorly received. As a result, it is important to think about how the recommendations will go over with your audience. Will the plan be received favorably? Or will it be questioned and challenged? Is the plan expected and safe? Or will it come as a surprise?

Although it is impossible to know how a plan will go over, it is usually possible to get a good idea. One way to do this is to ask probing questions in advance. Simply talking about a business with a senior executive will provide great context; if the conversation focuses on all the wonderful things that are happening, then you know that there may be a low appetite for radical change. If the conversation focuses on all the problems, then you know that there is a need for substantial and dramatic change.

If you're relatively confident that a plan will be supported, you can get to the recommendation very quickly; you are on safe ground. However, if you think your plan will be challenged, you will be better off building more slowly to the recommendation, explaining along the way why the obvious alternatives won't work. Jumping quickly to the recommendations in this case may well cause an immediate negative reaction; instead of listening fully to the recommendations your audience will probably just look for reasons to attack and reject the recommendation.

WHERE'S THE BEEF?

A good marketing plan should quickly address two key questions. First, what precisely is the recommendation? Second, why does the recommendation make sense?

All too often the actual recommendation (the "beef") is hard to find in the marketing plan; there is so much information, analysis, and detail swirling around the plan that it is very unclear what precisely is being recommended.

A marketing plan should very quickly get to the point and present the GOST, generally in this order. The topics follow logically. Strategic initiatives can only be considered once the objective is clear, and tactics can only be evaluated in light of the initiatives. As Conagra's Sergio Pereira observed, "If you don't agree on the objectives and the pillars, the rest of the discussion is useless."

There is much to be said for following the most basic of communication structures: tell your audience what you are going to tell them, tell it, and then tell them what you just told them. In other words, give a clear, concise overview of the plan, then outline the plan in detail, and then provide a clear and concise summary of what has been said. A marketing plan that follows this structure is on the right track; the plan should start with an introduction highlighting the key themes, then go through the plan in more detail, and then circle back to reinforce the key themes.

Being clear on the recommendations is essential. Equally important is having clear rationale: Why will the plan work? This is where analysis, facts, and detail play an essential role. The marketer must clearly construct a case explaining why the initiatives being recommended are the best possible choices for the business.

Your audience—the people reviewing and approving the plan—generally has a stake in the game; they want the plan to be successful, just as the manager does. In fact, the careers of the senior executives reviewing the plan usually depend on the marketing plan being successful. For this reason, your audience has a major incentive to study the plan with a critical eye, looking for shortcomings and better alternatives. As Dell's Kevin Rollins explained, "Occasionally our managers develop emotional connections to businesses that they really want to drive. But we make them prove the opportunity to us, and if we're not convinced, we don't move forward."[2]

Providing strong, balanced support is essential to selling the recommendation and building credibility in the organization. Most senior executives can see right through people who are just telling them what they want to hear. They want to see facts and be convinced. As Starwood's Barry Sternlicht observed,

> In order to build an organization, you have to be able to delegate, and in order to be able to delegate, you have to have confidence in the people working for you. You have to know that they're thorough in their research, that they gather all the facts they need, that they tell the truth about what they've found, that they form sensible opinions based on the data they've collected, and that they grasp the differences between fact and speculation.[3]

A good marketing plan clearly explains why the recommendations make sense and why they are the best recommendations for a particular situation. Facts and analysis then back up the recommendation.

Be a Storyteller

People who write great marketing plans tell a story; they find a way to connect different pieces of information and create a coherent, logical, simple narrative flow that ties the entire situation together.

Stories are powerful communication vehicles; stories are how people remember and process ideas. People have trouble remembering collections of facts. As a result, a marketing plan that reads like a story becomes memorable and logical.

Consider the following description of a business situation: "Our market share in 2005 was 43.1 percent, up from 42.6 percent in 2004. Share was 43.7 percent in 2006. Our key competitor had marketing spending totaling $37.1 million in 2006, up from $25.7 million in 2005 and $25.3 million in 2004. We spent $25.0 million on marketing in 2004 and $25.1 million in both 2005 and 2006."

Can you recall the market share in 2005 without looking? Do you even know whether the business is growing share or losing share? Probably not; people have trouble remembering details especially when they are presented in one large number-jumble.

It is far easier to remember this description: "Our business performed well between 2003 and 2006, growing share every year. In 2006, however, our key competitor responded, increasing marketing spending by almost 50 percent."

This description is much more powerful than the first description; it is clear and easy to remember. Perhaps more important, the second description drives toward action, drawing people to the obvious follow-up question, "So what do we do now?" The first description is hard to remember and doesn't lead anywhere.

Finding the narrative flow for a business is critical; you have to identify and tell a story that summarizes and supports the plan. The story then becomes the framework around which the plan is built, much like a skeleton supports flesh and muscle.

The ultimate challenge for someone writing a marketing plan is taking all the analysis, all the data, all the information, and all the ideas, and linking them together in a seamless flow. The very best marketing plans seem obvious and simple. The data all fits together; the points all make sense, they flow from one to the next, and the story leads you logically from one place to another. Great plans set up the situation and then logically, gradually pull you along.

A good story will summarize the entire plan in three or four sentences. It is very distilled and easy to follow. Most important, it sticks in the mind. Facts and details then make the plan robust and complete. You need both things: a story that is simple and easy to follow and facts that support the story.

As a result, once you finalize the recommendation, you must then find the story; this is the driving narrative flow for the plan. The core story summarizes the entire plan in three or four sentences. It is by definition simple and distilled.

A core story might look like this:

- The business is having a very good year with profit and revenue both up more than +10 percent.
- The strong results this year are due to the new products we launched in the first quarter.
- Our key challenge for the next year is continuing to grow despite flat category trends and the lack of a big new product launch.
- To drive the business next year, we recommend focusing on three things: invest in year 2 support for new product, expand advertising on the base business, and reduce costs by increasing efficiency.

The entire business situation and marketing plan is summarized in four simple, easy-to-follow statements.

For this reason, the ability to create a story is a core management skill; great leaders are able to summarize a situation and lay out the plan of attack.

Identifying the story is a challenge. Although it seems simple enough, actually finding the narrative thread is a significant challenge. Usually a team will have to go around and around looking for the proper flow. However, finding the core story is powerful; once you have it, the story serves as a roadmap for the entire marketing plan.

To find the core story, it is useful to try to summarize the entire marketing plan in three sentences. This is often called an "elevator pitch," because it's what you would say if you only had a minute or so to get your story across to someone in an elevator ride between floors. You can create the summary points by simply writing three or four sentences. Alternatively, you can talk to someone and try to summarize everything in a short statement. You can involve a group in the process, too, by gathering them together in a room and trying to summarize everything in three sentences on a flip chart.

Sometimes it takes a while to find the narrative flow; you have to try one approach, then another, then another, until one emerges.

For example, you might start with something like this:

- Our business is struggling; sales, profits, and share are all down versus prior year.
- Results are weak because raw material costs are up and competition is spending aggressively. In addition, our new product did not achieve its goals.
- To jump-start growth, we need to focus on attracting new customers through advertising and high-value promotions.
- Despite these activities, sales and profits will be down again next year. Share will be flat.

As you look at the summary, however, it is rather clear that the story doesn't work particularly well. How does the recommended plan address the issues? Why is a profit decline necessary? What happened to the new product, anyway? The flow simply doesn't make sense. The points don't connect to each other.

When a story doesn't flow properly, there are usually one or two problems. Either the story doesn't follow logically from one idea to the next, or the key premises are not right. In either case, though, you need to go back and rework the story.

Importantly, a story doesn't need to contain all the data and all the information. Indeed, this is basically impossible; the story simply provides the framework. In the story above, for example, it is worth considering the new product. Was that an important issue? Or was the new product flop something that happened but not a key driver? If so, there is no reason to include it in the core story. You shouldn't deny that it occurred, of course, but there is no reason to elevate it unless it plays a major role later in the plan. As they say in theater, if you introduce a gun in act one, someone should be shot in act two.

A revised version of the story above might go like this:

- Recent results have been disappointing due to aggressive moves by our competition; despite higher product costs, competitive spending is up.
- To be competitive in the market, we have to respond to these moves.
- Our recommended plan calls for increasing spending on both advertising and promotions to match the competitive moves.
- This will result in continued profit declines but a stabilization of market share.

This version of the plan is easier to follow; the points flow from one to the next, and there is a logical progression. The recommendation didn't change, and the financial information didn't change, but the overall story is now tighter and more compelling.

It's difficult to create a strong story unless you understand the business well and are confident in your recommendations. Boiling things down to the main points requires confidence. It is tempting to wonder, "But what if I just dropped out an important piece of information? What if I get a question about that? Will someone think I'm missing the main points?" In the earlier case, someone might start to worry, "I'm not discussing the new product. Won't that look bad? Don't I need to include that?"

Being confident enough to simplify a marketing plan is essential. As GE's Jack Welch observed, "Insecure managers create complexity. Frightened, nervous managers use thick, convoluted planning books and busy slides filled with everything they've known since childhood. Real leaders don't need clutter."[4]

Once the basic flow of a story is clear, you can move on to constructing the specific pages that will be in the plan. The core story sets the basic direction and functions as the outline.

In many cases, the story becomes the introduction, the agenda, the outline, and the summary. It is the glue that holds everything together.

It is critical to make sure the story comes through, as the plan gets longer and more robust. Each page or piece of information should fit somehow into the story. If a piece of data doesn't fit, it shouldn't be in the plan. If you are nervous about dropping it, you can put it in the appendix. Remember, of course, that few people actually ever look at an appendix.

When writing a full plan, it is essential that the headlines (in a presentation) or main points (in a written document) flow from one to the next. One helpful technique is "backing out" of your document by scrolling through and writing down just the headlines. In the best case, the headlines flow seamlessly, each one building on the prior headline and leading to the next headline.

Storyboarding is a technique that can be used to lay out a plan and make sure that each page flows from one to the next before you get too far in to the production process. This is the process of laying out the specific pages in a presentation to test the overall flow of the story as told by the headlines. Importantly, the focus is simply on the headlines, not on the detailed analysis. The goal is to check that one page flows logically to the next and that there aren't any obvious gaps in the story.

To storyboard, take a sheet of paper and draw three vertical lines and three horizontal lines, creating a series of nine squares (see exhibit 6.1).

Then, write a headline in each box, with a bit about what the page might eventually look like. If you think there will be a chart on a page, draw a rough picture of it. Each piece of paper, then, shows nine final pages in the presentation, so an 18-page presentation can be put on to just two pieces of paper. Don't include details; the goal is simply to see how the pages flow together (see exhibit 6.2).

Exhibit 6.1 Story Board Template

It is best to do this in pencil; the power of storyboarding is the ability to go back and revise the headlines and the flow based on an assessment of how the story is working. Is support lacking for a particular point? Add another page. Are there obvious questions the audience will ask? Make sure they are addressed. Does a chart seem out of place? Change its location or drop it.

The process of completing a storyboard forces a manager to be decisive; every page has to fit in, every piece of data has to contribute to the story. When the storyboard is done, the entire plan should seem simple and easy to follow. Creating the final document is then quite easy; the storyboard is the map.

CONVINCE ME

Ultimately, the goal of a marketing plan is to gain support. In general, marketing plans are written down to secure approval or get buy-in. After reading or hearing a plan, you want your audience to say, "Sure, this seems reasonable to me. Let's do it." In addition, if things go really well, you want to hear, "This is terrific. How can I help? What type of support do you need?"

For this to happen, a marketing plan has to be convincing. The plan has to persuade people that it will work and that it is the best possible solution. Considering the wide range of things a business can do, this is not always an easy task.

Once the story is clear in a plan, the task changes to providing the support points, or adding the data that backs up the recommendations. This is an important step in the process. A good story without support is just that: a good story. It won't persuade people on its own; you need data to prove your point and provide evidence.

This step can be time-consuming, as the relevant analyses and details must be written and inserted into the plan. However, if the story is clear, the process of adding the relevant data shouldn't be too time-consuming. A few things are worth remembering during this step.

Exhibit 6.2 Story Board Example

2007 is shaping up to be a terrific year —sales up 10% —profit up 10%	The powerful results are being driven by our new product —chart showing results	We believe we can continue to build our new product —chart showing opportunity
Our goal for next year is to accelerate our momentum —objective: +15% profit	Rising raw material costs will be a challenge —costs are up by 8% —this has major impact	We recommend focusing on three strategic initiatives —invest in new product —restructure trade promotion —reduce product costs
Our top priority is investing in year 2 support for our new product —new product is doing well —we can invest further	To drive new product, we will maintain launch year spending into year 2	We will focus activities on driving repeat business

Data, Data, Data

It is far more powerful to provide data proving a point than it is to simply state the point. An analysis that shows how margins have grown from 5 percent to 18 percent in five years is far more powerful than simply saying that margins have been increasing. Saying your competitor has been aggressive is fine, but presenting a chart illustrating how your competitor's advertising spending has gone from $52 million to $78 million in two years is convincing. Gary McCullough, CEO of Career Education, observed, "If you walk in and you've got the facts, you can usually carry the day."

Data always need sources; a piece of data without a source loses much of its value and credibility. Any important piece of data should come with a source, so it is clear where it came from. If you are to make an estimate, state that. If it is a solid piece of data, note that. This increases the impact of data substantially. In addition, you may well be asked about the source for a piece of data; if you cannot remember it, which will be likely, you will look careless. According to advertising executive Stuart Baum, sources are essential. "You will be asked. And you will not recall. And this will make you look dumb and careless. Or, that you do not trust the source."

Simplify

There are many ways to present the same source of data; you can write it, put it in a chart, or graph it. You can present a time series, showing changes over several years, or just look at a point in time. Using a fancy graphics program, you can put the data in a very elaborate chart.

The key is to find a way to present data that communicates clearly. The goal is for the data to be easily understood and clear.

It is possible and tempting to make things look complicated; virtually any piece of information can be made complicated and hard to follow. A highly abstract, technical bit of analysis may seem impressive, but if your audience can't easily understand it, the analysis adds no value. Consider the following two statements:

1. Two plus two equals four.
2. We built a model based on a multivariate regression that yielded an answer of four.

The first statement is simple, basic, and understandable. It's hard to lose people on the calculation. The second statement is complicated. It begs the questions, "How does the model work? What was the regression based on?" Without explaining exactly how the calculations work, the answer is simply a number. It requires a leap of faith: you have to believe the model to believe the number. The first calculation works much harder.

On a rare occasion, you may encounter an analysis that is too complex to simplify. In this case, you have two choices. First, you could spend the time to explain it, going through precisely where the analysis came from and what it means. Second, you might decide that it is not worth the time necessary to go through the analysis in detail and simply not include the chart.

Less Is More

Less data is generally better than more data. It is better to have a few power-ful reasons than a long collection.

Similarly, it is far better to space things out on several pages than try to load everything onto one page. Filling a page with type and figures might reduce the size of your presentation or recommendation, but it does this at great expense; the document becomes almost unreadable. If you find your-self using tiny type to fit your points onto a page, you need to pare down the points or add another page.

REFINEMENT AND REVISION

The final stage of writing a plan is refinement and revision. It is almost inevi-table that a first draft of a plan will not be perfect; the manager must go back to revise and refine.

Revising is an essential step in the process, because revisions will make the plan much stronger. As a result, it is important to leave time for it. It's also important to leave time for an outsider to read through the document. Many times an objective observer can point out holes and issues in a plan that the team can't see because they're too close to the subject matter.

During the revision process, it might become apparent that the plan sim-ply doesn't hold together; the story doesn't work or the data isn't strong enough to support the recommendations. In this case, the team may have to go back and revisit the objectives, strategic initiatives, and tactics.

The revising phase is also a time to get input and buy-in from cross-functional team members. The best marketing plans come with the full support of the entire business team; the plan is endorsed by the cross-functional group. The sales team thinks it will work, the operations people have no concerns, the market research people think the plan reflects their insights, and the finance people approve of the financial information included in the plan.

The easiest way to lose credibility in front of an executive is having a core team member introduce a concern or a major issue during the presentation. This instantly calls the entire plan into doubt, as executives begin to wonder whether the plan has been fully thought out and whether individual agen-das are trumping the overall business plan. It also makes the presenter look unprepared, and it is viewed as a sign of weak leadership. Worst of all, it looks like the team is hiding issues. This does enormous damage to the presenter's credibility and to the entire marketing plan.

As a result, a manager should involve the business team in writing and reviewing the plan. This is an art. A plan ultimately must have one pri-mary author; otherwise it feels disjointed. However, the author must share ownership of the content to be certain that the team agrees and that the plan reflects the different concerns. Kraft's Greg Wozniak noted that he was able to both involve the team and create a coherent plan: "The business team owned it, but it was me writing it."

An important insight for managers is this: The easiest way to get the team on board with a plan is to let them review the plan and make comments and suggestions, and then address their input. Conversely, there is no easier way to create dissent on the team than to ask for comments and then not respond to the suggestions.

*　*　*

A marketing plan has to be written, and written well, to be effective. A great plan should quickly get to the point, tell a simple story, and be supported by concrete, factual data and support.

CHAPTER 7

The Big Show

The marketing planning process almost always comes down to a single, pivotal meeting where the marketing manager stands up in front of a group of senior executives and, with his or her team, presents the marketing plan and answers questions. This is a critical moment.

If all goes well, the senior executives understand and support the plan. They are willing to provide resources and are enthusiastic about the future of the business. More importantly, they believe in the team that created the plan. The final approval may not come during the meeting itself, but it follows quickly enough.

If things don't go well, however, the outcome is much less positive; the senior executives don't follow or agree with the recommendations, and this leaves them with questions about the plan and, more significantly, the team.

It is sometimes painfully obvious when things go poorly; the team presenting the plan is drilled by question after question, and they struggle to respond coherently. Things can get rather ugly indeed. Once challenging questions come up, it can be difficult to keep the meeting on track. If things get very grim, the presenter may be forced to use their final lifeline, offering, "These are good issues. Why don't we regroup on them off-line?" This, of course, means that the remainder of the meeting is largely a waste of time, much like a race being run under a yellow flag. The meeting finally ends with a resounding thud, as one of the senior decision makers concludes, "Well, I think we will have to talk more about this."

Sometimes, though, a weak plan meeting is more subtle; the executives nod and eventually shuffle off. However, they are left unconvinced, and shortly after the meeting, they begin raising questions.

The presentation, then, matters a great deal. The ideas are important, and the written plan is a critical document, but actually presenting well is essential; a great marketing plan presented poorly will fall flat.

Creating a successful presentation seems straightforward: the team writes a good presentation and then someone gets up and presents it. However, a great presentation requires thought and consideration; it doesn't just happen.

No Surprises

The most important thing for a manager to remember is that much of the work in selling a recommendation takes place *before* the presentation takes place. In almost every case, a team should know how the plan will likely be received well before the presentation occurs. Similarly, the people listening to the plan should be familiar with the issues and know what sort of recommendations to expect. In an extreme case, everyone in the room may have already been through the presentation in advance of the meeting. This doesn't make the meeting a waste of time; the meeting provides the forum to discuss the recommendations, uncover potential issues, and ensure that everyone is on board with the plan.

No one wants to be caught off guard when it comes to a marketing plan presentation. As Unilever's David Hirschler observed, "Your manager doesn't want a big surprise the day of the presentation." Similarly, the team working on a plan doesn't want a surprise; uncovering a major issue during the marketing plan presentation makes everyone look bad.

To avoid surprises, the marketing team should identify key influencers several weeks before the plan presentation. These influencers may be cross-functional leaders in the organization, influential members of the business team, or outside consultants and vendors. Advertising agency executives, for example, are often highly influential. The marketing team should schedule individual or group meetings with the influencers to discuss the proposed recommendations. These discussions could be very informal, or they could be built around a formal review of the draft. The goals for the meeting are to get input on the recommendation and to secure support. If the marketing team isn't able to get buy-in, they should at least identify key issues. As Kraft's Greg Wozniak explained, "A lot of success is selling people on your ideas."

In addition to preselling to cross-functional teams, the team should also presell to the senior executives themselves. This is particularly important if the recommendation isn't likely to be what one or all of the executives were hoping or expecting to see. The marketing presentation should never surprise senior executives with bad news. A marketing plan presentation is not the time to announce that the business is performing poorly or that there is absolutely no chance of reaching the following year's profit goal. This sort of news will dominate the discussion, cause concern, and make it extremely unlikely that the plan will be approved.

If you have successfully presold a plan, you can be relatively confident about the meeting; it will probably go well. This is a powerful place to be, because you can then focus on making sure everyone agrees with the plan and you have access to all the resources needed to make the plan successful.

Setting the Stage

Any presentation is a dog and pony show. It is a bit of theater. As a result, setting the stage is important. If the stage isn't set correctly, the show won't go smoothly, and the audience will notice. The goal, then, is to think about the stage well in advance and to set it thoughtfully.

Gather the Right Crowd

It is hard to have a great meeting if the right people are not there. For a marketing plan presentation to really work, the key players have to be present. This will generally include senior executives and key influencers.

Understanding your audience is critical when thinking about who needs to be present. Some executives love large groups; they welcome the entire team and want to be the center of attention. There is an excitement and drama that comes with a full room, and they warm to this. For people such as this, large meetings work best; a crowded room is ideal. Indeed, these executives may actually be uncomfortable in a small group.

Other executives are far less comfortable in large groups. If there are too many people in the room, some people won't ask questions and discuss issues. For people such as this, it is best to have a very small meeting, with just a few people, perhaps five or six people in total. Having a large meeting will be relatively unproductive, because issues won't surface and questions won't be answered.

At one point in my career I reported to a general manager who was extremely uncomfortable with large groups; I quickly learned that the best way to take him through a marketing plan was to simply sit down in his office and flip through it, one on one.

Prepare the Room

People make judgments quickly. The moment people walk in the conference room, they are forming opinions about your plan and about your team. If the team is scrambling to get ready, for example, your audience might start thinking the team isn't prepared. If there aren't enough chairs, your audience might conclude the team doesn't plan well.

It is important to prepare a room before any meeting, and especially before a marketing plan presentation. You don't want to learn that the projector doesn't work two minutes before you're supposed to start; it looks sloppy. Your goal is to set the stage for the plan presentation, to think ahead, and to make sure that the obvious details have been covered. This sends the signal that you and your team are thoughtful, organized, and ready.

The first step in preparing the presentation room is to make sure everything is technically functional. This seems obvious, but all too often the computer doesn't work, or the hookup to the projector fails, or the bulb in the overhead projector is out. How many times have you sat through a meeting where the presenter clicks futilely away at the screen with his or her clicker, only to have the projector fail to cooperate? You don't want that to happen to you at this critical juncture in the marketing plan process.

Other small details are equally as important. Are there enough chairs? Is the temperature right? These details might not seem to warrant the attention of a marketing manager, but your audience will take cues from everything around them during the presentation. The old adage holds true: you never get a second chance to make a first impression. A presenter who struggles to get the projector working or isn't ready at the designated time looks disorganized, and this hurts overall credibility.

Pay Attention

It's critical to get the right people in the right seats. The key executives, the one or two people who will have the most influence on the acceptance of the plan, should occupy the most prominent seats. It's a good idea to put these executives wherever they will be most comfortable, and surround them with people who make them feel comfortable. If the key decision makers are comfortable, they will be more likely to support your plan.

SHOW YOUR CONFIDENCE

Perhaps the most important element of a marketing plan presentation is the confidence of the presenter. Senior executives *need* to see confidence in the presenter. A nervous and insecure presenter simply makes everyone feel uncomfortable, and it makes the team and all its hard work look weak.

Senior executives analyze two things in a marketing plan presentation. First, they look at the plan itself. Will it work? Are there any major flaws? Then they look at the team and the team leader, wondering whether they can trust the recommendations they're being given. According to one marketing executive, senior managers ask, "How good a person is this? Does he know what's really going on? And what is he going to do about it?" For these reasons, projecting confidence during the presentation is essential.

The challenge is to be confident without being too confident. As *Advertising Age* columnist Bob Garfield observed, "Think about the advice they give roofers and iron workers. You've got to feel comfortable up there, or else you'll fall. But you can't feel too comfortable, or else you'll forget where you are...and fall."[1]

Confidence comes from three places: practice, knowing the business, and having a firm grasp of the facts.

Practice

Presenting a marketing plan is much like telling a story; it gets better the more you do it. As Herminia Ibarra and Kent Lineback wrote in the *Harvard Business Review*, "Any veteran storyteller will agree that there's no substitute for practicing in front of a live audience. Tell and retell your story; rework it like a draft of an epic novel until the 'right' version emerges."[2]

The best way to become confident presenting a marketing plan is to practice. Assemble test audiences and present it again and again. Listen for the questions and ask people to search for the issues. The more times you do something successfully, the more confident you will become.

Often, these practice presentations will uncover opportunities to improve the presentation and, sometimes, even the plan itself. If the basic presentation doesn't work, if it doesn't hold together, the problem might be in the written document, or it might be in the plan itself. A presentation that doesn't work is sometimes a warning sign of a bad plan.

Know the Business

The most powerful way to project confidence is to really understand the business and the recommendation. If you are 100 percent certain that you know the business and you believe fully that your recommendation is sound, then confidence will naturally follow.

To some extent, confidence is the natural result of a good planning process. If a manager analyzed a business in depth, identified the most powerful strategic initiatives and tactics, confirmed the financials, and then pulled it all together into a compelling recommendation, confidence will be a natural result.

Find the Facts

There is nothing as powerful as facts to provide confidence. Opinion and subjective observation are dangerous territory; in the end, a question of opinions usually is decided by seniority or forcefulness. A presenter can't count on either. Facts, however, can be rock solid bits of truth that hammer home a point without question.

A great way to build confidence is to know the facts. When pressed, if you have facts to drop back on, you'll be well covered. If a senior executive offers an opinion and you're able to counter it with a fact, that executive must adjust course; he or she can't just wish the fact away.

It is particularly important to understand the data and numbers forward and backward. A manager who can't explain the figures looks self-conscious and confused, not confident. Usually, not being able to explain the figures is a sign that the analysis isn't complete. As Daniel Okrent, Public Editor at the *New York Times*, wrote in a recent piece, "Number fumbling arises, I believe, not from mendacity but from laziness, carelessness, or lack of comprehension."[3] This is another reason to keep the analysis in a marketing plan simple; it is easy to explain.

But importantly, presenters don't have to know *all* the facts, and they shouldn't even try to. It is simply impossible to know all the facts on a business. Even attempting to do so will likely cause confusion and a cluttered mental state, not the mindset you want on the day of a key presentation.

A manager just has to know a few critical facts that support key points in the presentation. Facts such as this provide points of refuge when questions arise. They also send a strong impression to the audience.

Consider, for example, what happens when a presenter is questioned about the price sensitivity of the business, and he or she states without pause, "This business just isn't that price sensitive. More than 62 percent of our customers believe that our products are worth paying a premium for, and our price elasticity is 0.71, well below the industry average of 1.06." Undoubtedly, the presenter will likely carry the point; there are strong facts that support the argument. More importantly, the presenter is sending a clear message: "I know this business inside and out."

When preparing for a presentation, it is useful to identify and memorize seven key facts. These should be precise and unquestionable; you should know the source and the methodology behind the figure. Then, during the meeting, you can use the facts in the presentation or, more powerfully, you can use the facts when answering a question.

GET SOME ALTITUDE

Great presenters follow the altitude principle, a theory of aviation that goes like this: It is far better to encounter turbulence when you have lots of altitude than when you are flying close to the group.

In other words, an airplane flying along at 35,000 feet can encounter a lot of turbulence and continue safely on its way; the plane can drop 5,000 or even 10,000 feet and still be high above the ground. In extreme cases, people may be thrown about and injured, but the plane usually survives and reaches its destination. Conversely, an airplane just taking off or about to land must be far more careful about turbulence. When flying at an altitude of 200 feet, a plane that drops just 201 feet due to turbulence will crash and burn. This is unfortunate and true. It is partly why most airplane crashes occur during takeoff and landing.

This theory is useful when thinking about a presentation, too. It is far better to encounter turbulence in the middle of a presentation than at the beginning or the end. If there is something in your presentation that you think will be controversial, it's best to put it in the middle. At the start of a presentation, the team is settling in and your audience is becoming familiar with the issues. "Takeoff" is the time to present well-known, established, and safe material. Then, once you have gotten some momentum, once your audience is flying high with you, nodding their heads in agreement, you can move on to the controversial material. At this point a bit of turbulence in the form of questions and debate is not a bad thing. Near the end of the presentation, however, it is again time to minimize turbulence; you don't want to finish with questions and send people off with doubts.

BRING IT TO LIFE

The goal in a marketing plan presentation is secure enthusiastic support. To do this, a manager has to win both heart and head. Presenting a credible, solid plan that rationally makes sense is good but not sufficient; it might win over the head, but it won't win the heart.

To win the heart a manager has to project excitement and enthusiasm. To really sell a plan and mobilize an organization, a leader must win the rational argument and the emotional argument. Great pages and a well-structured presentation can leverage the data, but the presentation also must exude flair and energy. As Bill Gates explained in his 2007 commencement address at Harvard University, "You can't get people excited unless you can help them see and feel the impact."[4]

Marketing plan presentations always benefit from props and show-and-tell. Simply explaining what you want to do is ineffective compared to actually showing what you want to do.

Plans also benefit from the use of a theme or slogan; this makes the plan catchy and memorable. One marketing executive wrote a plan about a business turnaround and called it, "The Year of the Phoenix." As marketing veteran Roland Jacobs observed, "You've got to have something to make it memorable. It's a silly little thing, but it makes a difference." Another executive handed four toy cars to each person in the audience: a Hummer, a Mini Cooper, a minivan, and a sedan, to make the point that customers have very different motivations, and trying to reach everyone at the same time would never work.

* * *

There is something incredibly powerful about seeing a team stand up and present a well thought out marketing plan. A good marketing plan presentation creates excitement and energy. However, this only occurs with thoughtful planning, preparation, and practice.

CHAPTER 8

Marketing Plan Template

There is no single format for a marketing plan and no one perfect model. Some marketing plans are written documents, and some are presentations. Some are lengthy and detailed, while others are short and concise. Some marketing plans are never formally written down; they are scribbled on a napkin in a restaurant.

More than anything, a marketing plan needs to fit the situation. A complicated business will probably require a more detailed plan than a simple business; a marketing plan for Microsoft Office will obviously need to be longer and more detailed than a marketing plan for a small neighborhood restaurant. A troubled business may require a longer plan than a successful business; the task of credibly laying out the plan for a struggling business is usually more difficult than for a successful business; the plan for the successful business will likely recommend a continuation of current strategic initiatives.

At the core, though, almost all good marketing plans follow the same basic flow. This is true whether they are written or presented, whether long or short. The general sequence of things is usually the same.

What follows are two tools to help craft a breakthrough marketing plan. The first is a general marketing plan outline, explaining what should be in a plan and how it should generally flow. This can be used for written plans. The second is a detailed, page-by-page template for presented plans. The template shows precisely what the pages in a marketing plan presentation should look like.

One note of caution: Both the outline and the template should be used as starting points. Indeed, providing a template for a marketing plan is a little dangerous; the risk is that people will simply fill in the pages instead of thinking about the situation facing the business or giving adequate time to crafting the story that explains where the business is at the moment, which justifies the plan of attack. The goal, ultimately, is not to follow a template—it is to create a marketing plan that lays out the course for the business, is supported by data and facts, and then delivers strong business results.

MARKETING PLAN OUTLINE

The following outline presents the key parts of a marketing plan. This can be used whether the plan is a presentation or a written document. It can also be used whether the plan is short and concise or more detailed; the sections simply vary in size and rigor.

Title Page

A marketing plan should always start with a title page. This is completely obvious but all too often overlooked.

A title page should include the name of the business, the date the plan was completed or presented, the people on the team, and most importantly, the title. The title is usually something like this: British Airways 2008–2009 Marketing Plan.

Each element is important. The name of the business is of course essential; you have to know what business is being discussed. The date is also important, because in most cases there will be many versions of a marketing plan floating around, each one updated and revised slightly. If the date isn't on the plan, it can be hard to determine which one is the most recent version.

Putting the names of the team on the title page does three different things. First, it clarifies who precisely created the plan. This is usually obvious at the time when a plan is presented. However, marketing plans tend to hang around for years and years. Five years after the plan, it is often hard to figure out who was involved at the time. With names on the title pages, it is clear who worked on it, and then it becomes easy to follow up with those people if need be.

Second, including names on the title page cements commitment from the team; it is hard to disagree with a plan when your name is on the cover. This can be very powerful. People often take deep interest in a document when their name is on it. There is no better way to ensure support.

Third, including names on the title page also makes it easy to share the credit. It is a reward, in a sense, to the people who spent time thinking about and creating the plan. People generally like to be recognized. Without their name on a plan, people may feel the need to actually present something in the final meeting to show everyone that they, too, contributed to the plan and were part of the process. This can lead to choppy and disjointed presentations.

Executive Summary

When I was a child, I was a member of my local 4-H club. I raised pigs and sheep, caught butterflies, and built birdhouses. Moreover, each year I gave a presentation in the public speaking program. One year I gave a talk about washing chickens, another year I discussed raising ducks, and another year I explored the topic of collecting beetles.

One of the things I learned from those presentations is the power of a good summary. If I started with a short summary of my key points, then the presentation usually went well, and I received a blue ribbon every time. The famous line from *English 101* is really true: say what you're going to say, say it, and then say what you just said. I also learned that bringing a chicken to a presentation is a good way to win over your audience, though that lesson is a bit harder to apply in the corporate world. Of course, if you think creatively I bet you can bring something that would have a similar impact.

Similarly, marketing plans benefit from a good summary. If you lead with a short summary of the plan, you're off to a very good start. This is why a marketing plan should always start with an executive summary. It should be short and focused, highlighting the key parts of the plan, including the goals and objectives and strategic initiatives. In a presentation, the executive summary should be no more than two pages, with four or five points on each page.

The summary does several things. Most importantly, it gets the point across. Many people can't focus for long periods. As a result, if you put the main points of your recommendation at the end, many people won't pay attention. Putting the most important points first increases the chance that people will actually be paying attention.

An executive summary also helps your audience, because it gives them a sense of what is to come. This helps people to figure out how to listen to the presentation. If the plan seems reasonable and expected, for example, an executive may decide to say very little, provide some encouragement, and stay away from the details; there is no need to debate the fine points of an analysis if the overall conclusion makes sense. Why waste the time and energy? If the plan is a major change or a big surprise, however, an executive will quickly see the need to pay attention, making sure to understand the analysis and the recommendation, and see if there are holes in the logic.

The executive summary also sets the tone for the presentation. If the business is in great shape and the plan simply builds on this success, then the summary should set a tone of prudent confidence and optimism. If the business is in trouble and the plan is a dramatic change from the past, then the tone should be serious and urgent.

The only time a marketing plan should not start with a summary of the plan is when the recommendation is so controversial that putting it up front might cause a strongly negative reaction. In this case, the plan would still have an executive summary at the start, but the meat of the recommendation, the controversial part, would be farther back in the document. The introduction should simply set up the need for bold and innovative thinking but not get into the specifics; those come later.

Agenda

An agenda or table of contents is important even in a small plan, simply to let people know what is coming up and how the presentation will flow.

Letting people see what's ahead is critical. For example, senior executives will usually want to see the financial implications, so it's important to tell them when the topic will be addressed. Otherwise they'll probably go searching for the financial information or get progressively nervous that it won't be discussed at all. Without a clear agenda, people may feel the need to jump in and ask about things that will be coming later in the presentation, forcing a presenter to constantly reply, "We'll be getting to that later in the presentation."

In a presentation, the agenda can also serve as an organizing device, nicely dividing sections of the presentation.

The table of contents is best positioned after the one-page summary; the energy and excitement is in the summary; the table of contents comes to life once the audience has a sense for where things are heading.

State of the Business

The first step in building a house is laying the foundation; this is what the house is built on. Without a foundation you can't make a lot of progress. This is also true with marketing plans; you need to lay the foundation before you can construct the plan.

A good foundation in a marketing plan ensures that there is a common understanding of the business. There should be three things in this section of the plan: the vision and positioning, an update on recent results, and the business challenge.

Any marketing plan needs to take into account the vision and positioning on a brand; taking up the prices on a brand positioned on value, for example, will be very risky. Similarly, launching a fast sports car makes little sense for an automobile brand based on safety.

The vision and brand positioning should not be anything new; it should simply be a review of what is already known and agreed upon by the team. If you don't have a positioning on a particular brand, for example, you should figure it out before including it in the plan; putting a new positioning into a marketing plan is a good way to derail the discussion entirely, because positioning discussions can go on and on and on.

A marketing plan must include an update on how the business is doing; it must be written with an understanding of results. A business that is doing well faces certain issues, and a business not doing well faces very different issues. Being clear on this is important; everyone reviewing the plan has to agree on how the business is doing before reviewing the plan, just as physicians have to agree on a diagnosis before debating the correct treatment course.

The recent results section should be brief and, again, should not present completely new information. Announcing that the business is doing much better than expected will simply derail the discussion; people will focus on understanding why things are going so well.

Finally, the foundation should identify the key challenge or two facing the business. In the big picture, what is the main issue the plan has to address? The challenge might be accelerating growth, building margins in a declining category, or battling a competitive entrant. Clarity on this is critical.

Every business faces challenges. Businesses that are doing poorly of course face the challenge of turning around the business. Very simply, how will management get the business on the right track? Businesses that are doing well also face challenges, and in some ways these are more difficult. How will the business continue to grow? What will sustain the momentum over time?

The challenge section is important because it lays the groundwork for the rest of the plan. Every point in the section should be considered, because the recommended plan builds off this material. Importantly, every issue identified in the set-up should be addressed in the plan.

In theater, there is a general rule that if a gun appears in act one, then someone needs to shoot the gun in act two. Otherwise, why include the gun in act one at all? The same applies in writing a marketing plan; if an issue is mentioned in the set-up, it should be addressed somewhere in the plan.

The business challenge section of the plan should be short and focused. In a presentation, the positioning should take a page, the results review should take one or two pages, and the challenge should take one or two pages. The goal is not to present mounds of data about the business. The goal is to simply highlight how the business is performing and the challenges the plan needs to address, to be sure everyone is on the same page.

Objectives

The objectives section should present the one or two key objectives for the upcoming period. One objective should almost always be centered on profit, and sometimes that is sufficient. In most cases, however, a business will have another objective or two in addition to profit, such as increasing market share, improving brand perception, or establishing a presence in a new market.

The objectives should not be a surprise for the audience; these should be communicated in advance, and this section should be a review, confirming that the objectives are correct. This is sort of a routine check, much as flight attendants do a destination check before closing the plane doors.

Indeed, if there is disagreement on the objectives, there is no point in proceeding with the rest of the plan; a marketing plan created to achieve one set of objectives will rarely be appropriate to achieve a different set of objectives.

The objectives section should be short; in a presentation it should be at most one or two pages.

Strategic Initiatives and Tactics

The strategic initiatives and tactics section should lay out the three or four more important initiatives and the tactics associated with each one. This is a critical part of the plan; this is where the plan gets around to the actual recommendation of what should be done.

There are two different ways to present strategic initiatives and tactics. The first way is to review all of the strategic initiatives first, and then get into the tactics. This approach is good because it keeps the focus on the initiatives; all the big moves can be explained and justified before getting into tactical matters. In addition, this makes the overall plan easy to review. The limitation, however, is that the plan can be a little cumbersome because you have to discuss each initiative twice, once to agree on the initiatives and then, later on, to look at how the initiative will be implemented.

The second way to present this material is to take each initiative in turn, discussing the first initiative and the tactics associated with it before proceeding on to the second initiative. This approach tightly links the initiative and the tactics. The challenge with this approach is that it can make the total plan hard to see; the tactics are mixed in with the initiatives, so it is possible to get lost in the tactics before understanding all the initiatives.

Regardless of how the plan is organized, the tactical information should always be summarized; there is not time to go through all the tactical details. This is true on even the simplest of businesses. A discussion of tactics can go on and on and on; understanding something as simple as a modest packaging change can take a very long time. In the plan presentation, the focus should remain on the big moves. What must happen to make each strategic initiative successful?

This section can be summarized with the GOST summary chart, showing the goals and objectives, initiatives, and plans on the same page.

Financial Implications

Every marketing plan needs a section on financials; failing to link the plan to the numbers is a common problem and one that almost inevitably creates issues. Strategy is great and ideas are wonderful, but the numbers have to work for the plan to be convincing.

At the end of the day, a business has to deliver profits; after all, that's the main objective for any for-profit venture. A flashy plan that makes enormous sense but has no chance of delivering the financial targets is of little use. A business has to make money.

The financial section of a marketing plan should present a topline profit and loss statement, showing sales, spending, and profit in a summary manner. The financial section should address a simple question: if we execute this plan, what is likely to happen to the financials of the business?

Importantly, the financial section should link back to the objectives. In most cases, profit will be one of the objectives. In the financial section, then, the projected results should be compared to the objectives. Will this plan deliver the goal? Will it fall short? Will it over-deliver the goal?

It is often useful to include the opportunities and risks page in this section, to highlight the risks facing a business and the likely outcome, and the opportunities that might materialize.

The challenge in the financial section is to provide enough information to indicate how the plan will impact the financial outlook without becoming bogged down in the details; a marketing plan is not a budgeting process. In general, a summary income statement is sufficient, showing the most important parts.

Milestones

This section presents key milestones for the business. It answers a rather basic question: how do we know if we are on track? To get great execution, a business needs milestones to monitor progress and indicate if things are coming together.

A business can't have 50 milestones. The focus of this section is to highlight a few key things to watch that will indicate whether the plan is on track or not.

If a marketing plan calls for a big new product introduction, for example, then key milestones might include getting positive test results, developing good advertising, and gaining a certain amount of distribution. Alternatively, if cost reductions are important, the milestones might highlight that by the end of the first quarter the ideas have to be clear.

Executive Summary Reprise

A marketing plan should finish with a reprise of the executive summary; this is when you tell them what you told them. People often neglect the end of the plan, figuring that by the time the end appears everyone will be so tired that it is best to simply walk off and get back to work. This is absolutely not the case; the summary, or the end of a marketing plan, is critical. After all the plan detail, the challenge is to bring the audience back to the main points so that everyone leaves with the core messages top of mind.

One approach that works well is to simply copy the executive summary from the beginning of the plan, so the same material opens and closes the plan. This is very effective because it provides strong bookends. It also makes the summary the most important part in the plan, which, of course, it is.

MARKETING PLAN TEMPLATE

The marketing plan template that follows can serve as a basic guide to laying out a marketing plan. Remember, though, that it is just a starting point; managers should modify it as needed to be sure that it tells a story. Completing a template is helpful, but it will only work if the plan tells a compelling story.

Exhibit 8.1   Marketing Plan Template

2009 Marketing Plan
—Product—

Date
Presenters
Location

Agenda

---

1. Executive Summary
2. State of the Business
3. Objectives/Strategic Initiatives/Tactics
4. Financial Implications
5. Milestones

2009 Marketing Plan

Agenda

---

1. Executive Summary
2. State of the Business
3. Objectives/Strategic Initiatives/Tactics
4. Financial Implications
5. Milestones

2009 Marketing Plan

Executive Summary

This page should summarize the overall plan in several bullets.
The executive summary should be no more than two pages.

2009 Marketing Plan

Agenda

1. Executive Summary
2. State of the Business
3. Objectives/Strategic Initiatives/Tactics
4. Financial Implications
5. Milestones

2009 Marketing Plan

Vision and Product Positioning

This page should present the vision and positioning. This should not be new information; it should simply be a reminder.

2009 Marketing Plan

Recent Results

This page should provide an update on the business to set the stage for the plan to follow.

Key things to address: *1. How is the business performing?*

                               2. What are the key drivers of recent results?

In general, the information presented here should not be new; the page serves as a recap of the current situation.

If needed, this section could include several pages.

2009 Marketing Plan

Business Challenge

This page should summarize the core challenge facing the business going forward.

The challenge will usually be linked to the results recap.

For example, if results have been weak due to competitive spending, the core challenge may well be how to deal with the competitive situation.

2009 Marketing Plan

Agenda

---

1. Executive Summary
2. State of the Business
3. Objectives/Strategic Initiatives/Tactics
4. Financial Implications
5. Milestones

2009 Marketing Plan

Objectives

This page should present the objectives for the business, such as revenue growth or profit growth.

The objectives should not be a surprise to the audience.

It is best to have only one or two objectives.

2009 Marketing Plan

Strategic Initiatives

This section presents the strategic initiatives that will drive the business. What needs to happen to achieve the objective?

Strategic initiatives are always actions, such as driving trial on a new product or building loyalty among heavy users.

The section should explain why the initiative is important.

It is best to have three or four strategic initiatives.

This section could include several pages, perhaps one page per initiative.

2009 Marketing Plan

Tactics

This section presents the tactics supporting each strategic initiative along with rationale.

For example, a strategic initiative of building awareness might have tactics such as advertising and local events.

Each initiative should have tactics and each tactic should be linked to an initiative.

This section can be split onto several pages. For example, each initiative could have a separate page.

2009 Marketing Plan

One Page Plan Summary

Goals/Objectives   **Strategic Initiatives**   **Tactics**

Primary objective

Secondary objective

Strategic Initiative 1

Strategic Initiative 2

Strategic Initiative 3

—Tactic
—Tactic

—Tactic
—Tactic
—Tactic

—Tactic
—Tactic

2009 Marketing Plan

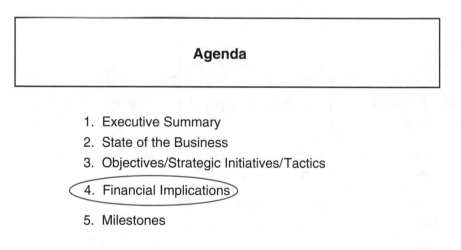

Agenda

1. Executive Summary
2. State of the Business
3. Objectives/Strategic Initiatives/Tactics
4. Financial Implications
5. Milestones

2009 Marketing Plan

Financial Implications

This section should bridge to the financials.

Ideally, the page should lay out the implications for spending and show how the business will hit the objective.

Final budgets should not be included.

2009 Marketing Plan

Risks and Contingencies

Risks   Contingencies

This section should show the risks to the plan and the contingencies. What might go wrong? If this happens, what is the backup plan?

2009 Marketing Plan

Agenda

1. Executive Summary
2. State of the Business
3. Objectives/Strategic Initiatives/Tactics
4. Financial Implications
5. Milestones

2009 Marketing Plan

Milestones

Milestone   Date

What needs to happen for the plan to work? What are the key dates?
There should only be a few milestones.

2009 Marketing Plan

Executive Summary

It is good to finish the presentation by repeating the executive summary; this lets you reinforce the key points.

2009 Marketing Plan

Breakthrough Marketing
Plan Example

The marketing plan that follows is a hypothetical plan written for Flahavan's, an Irish food company.

E. Flahavan & Sons Limited is an old, well-established company in Ireland. The company dates back to the 1700s, when an oats mill was built in Kilmacthomas, County Waterford. The mill was powered by the nearby river Mahon and today the company still generates electricity from the river in an environmentally friendly way to help power the plant. Flahavan's is a private company, now in its sixth generation of family ownership. This makes it Ireland's oldest family-owned food company.

Flahavan's is the leading brand of porridge in Ireland, with more than 50 percent of the total market. The company only produces products under the Flahavan's brand, operating as a branded house. Virtually all of Flahavan's sales are from the Irish market; the company has a limited presence in other countries.

The marketing plan that follows is an illustrative example of a plan that Flahavan's might develop, written in a presentation format. I have changed all the specific information to maintain confidentiality. The plan is short, focused, and action-oriented. It is a simple plan, as marketing plans should be. It also includes support for all the key recommendations. It is a good model to follow.

Exhibit 9.1   Marketing Plan Example

2009 Marketing Plan
Flahavan's

This plan is purely an
example. The data,
people, and strategies
discussed in this plan
are all illustrative.

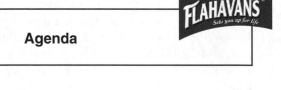

John Smith, Susan Johnson, and Mark Rogers
October 15, 2008
Dublin, Ireland

Agenda

1. Executive Summary
2. State of the Business
3. Objectives/Strategic Initiatives/Tactics
4. Financial Implications
5. Milestones

Flahavan's 2009 Marketing Plan

Agenda

1. Executive Summary
2. State of the Business
3. Objectives/Strategic Initiatives/Tactics
4. Financial Implications
5. Milestones

Flahavan's 2009 Marketing Plan

Flahavan's is Poised for Further Growth

- Flahavan's has delivered strong results, with 2008 profits up +8%, due to robust category growth and a modest price increase

- Flahavan's has two goals for 2009: increase profit by +9% and maintain share of the porridge category at 62.1%

- The 2009 marketing plan is focused on three big initiatives
  —Continue to drive category growth by promoting health benefits
  —Launch quick oats portable cups to address growing need for convenience and build margins
  —Evaluate new snacking line and expansion into U.S. market

- The primary risk facing the business is that product costs may increase more than expected. If this occurs we will increase list prices to maintain margins

Flahavan's 2009 Marketing Plan

118

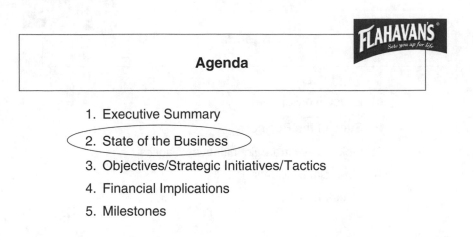

Agenda

1. Executive Summary
2. State of the Business
3. Objectives/Strategic Initiatives/Tactics
4. Financial Implications
5. Milestones

Flahavan's 2009 Marketing Plan

Flahavan's Positioning and Vision

• Vision:

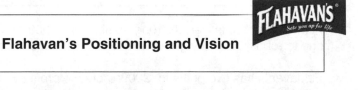

We will be the leader in Oat Based Products

• Positioning:

To busy, active women in Ireland, Flahavan's is the brand of breakfast food that is most nutritious because Flahavan's is natural and high in fiber and has a low glycaemic index

Flahavan's 2009 Marketing Plan

2008 will be an Excellent Year for Flahavan's

- The Flahavan's business is performing well across all measures
  —2008 sales volume will be up by +4% with revenues up +6%
  —Profits will finish the year up +8%
  —Volume share will be up +0.8 points to 62.1%

- Strong results are due to category growth, a price increase, and reduced competitive activity
  —The porridge category is forecast to grow by +3% this year due to an increased focus on nutrition among consumers
  —Our +2.5% list price increase contributed to revenue and profit growth and allowed us to increase advertising by +11%
  —O'Briens, our key competitor, followed our price increase and reduced marketing spending in an apparent bid to boost short-term profits

Flahavan's 2009 Marketing Plan

The Challenge for Flahavan's is to Drive Continued Category Growth

- The porridge category has grown by an average of +4% in volume over the last five years. This growth has been the primary profit driver for our business

- However, there is evidence that category growth is beginning to slow

Irish Porridge Category
Volume Change

2005	+6%
2006	+6%
2007	+4%
2008 Forecast	+3%
2008 1 Half	+4%
2008 2 Half Forecast	+1%

- Maintaining category growth is critical for continued profit growth on the business

Flahavan's 2009 Marketing Plan

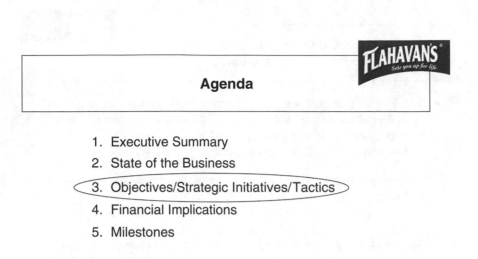

Agenda

1. Executive Summary
2. State of the Business
3. Objectives/Strategic Initiatives/Tactics
4. Financial Implications
5. Milestones

Flahavan's 2009 Marketing Plan

Flahavan's is Focused on Driving Strong Profit Growth in 2009 while Maintaining Share

2009 Objectives

1. Increase profits by +9%

2. Maintain market share at 62.1%

Flahavan's Results

	Profit Change (%)	Share (%)
2006	+2	60.8
2007	+4	61.3
2008 Forecast	+8	62.1
2009 Objective	+9	62.1

Flahavan's 2009 Marketing Plan

To Drive Growth in 2009, the Business will Focus on Three Strategic Initiatives

<u>2009 Strategic Initiatives</u>

- Continue to drive category growth by promoting health benefits

- Launch quick oats portable cups to address growing need for convenience and build margins

- Evaluate new snacking line and expansion into U.S. market

Flahavan's 2009 Marketing Plan

Promoting the Category is Essential

- There is an opportunity to further grow the category
  —Only 48% of households currently serve porridge
  —Porridge makes up only 41% of breakfasts in households that serve porridge

- Health is the main opportunity for driving additional category growth
  —Health concerns are increasing
  —There is limited awareness of the health benefits of porridge

% of Irish Women

	2005	2006	2007	2008
Concerned about Health	42	48	47	52
Aware of Health Benefit of Porridge	31	38	39	41

Flahavan's 2009 Marketing Plan

To Drive the Category we will Expand Advertising and PR Programs

- Advertising has proven to be effective at growing the category
  —The category grows significantly faster when we advertise

- PR is a major opportunity to expand awareness of health benefits
  —2008 efforts have generated 42 major news stories about health benefits of the category

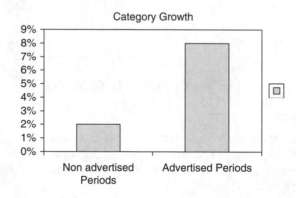

Flahavan's 2009 Marketing Plan

Launching Portable Cups will Address Convenience and Build Margins

- Convenience is a significant issue in the category
  —The #1 reason people do not eat porridge in the morning is convenience, or lack of time
  —Convenience will likely become more important for our consumers going forward due to increases in dual income households

- Quick oats portable cups addresses convenience need
  —Portable cups product is simple to prepare: just add hot water
  —Concept received strong concept and product test scores
  —61% of consumers agreed the product was more convenient

- Margins on quick oats cups are higher than our traditional progress oatlets1kg pack

Flahavan's 2009 Marketing Plan

The 2009 Plan Includes a Launch of Portable Cups in the Second Quarter

- Announce product line in first quarter with a second quarter start ship

- Launch a three item line: original, strawberry, and brown sugar
  —Ensure substantial shelf presence
  —Provide variety for consumers

- Support heavily
  —Build awareness through advertising in second and third quarter
  —Drive trial with sampling program and in-store coupons
  —Cross-sell new products on existing items

Flahavan's 2009 Marketing Plan

Exploring Longer Term Growth Opportunities is Critical

- Our business is currently reliant on one category. Slowing category growth or increased competition will impact overall growth rates

- Snacking is a compelling growth opportunity
  —Huge and growing market
  —A logical extension for our business
  —A good fit for our health positioning

- The U.S. market warrants consideration
  —An enormous opportunity: more than $1 billion in revenue
  —A growing market
  —Lots of potential: similar sized companies have been able to launch successful niche products

Flahavan's 2009 Marketing Plan

Flahavan's 2009 Marketing Plan Summary

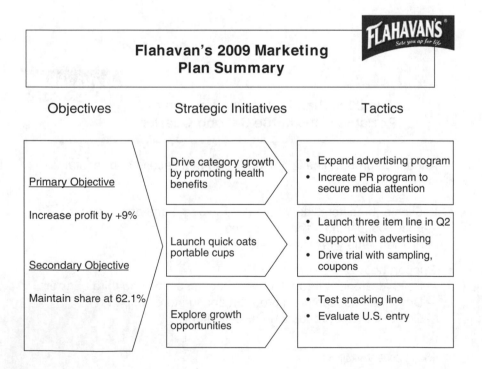

Flahavan's 2009 Marketing Plan

Agenda

1. Executive Summary
2. State of the Business
3. Objectives/Strategic Initiatives/Tactics
4. Financial Implications
5. Milestones

Flahavan's 2009 Marketing Plan

Building Category and New Cup Line will Require Additional Spending

- Increasing the category will require sharp increase in media and PR spending

- New cup line will require advertising and promotional support

- Product costs are expected to be up slightly

	2008	2009	Change	
Category Growth	+3%	+5%	+2 pts	Up due to category build initiative
Flahavan's Share	62.1%	62.1%	—	Flat share
Flahavan's Volume (MM kgs)	50.0	52.5	+5%	Growing due to category expansion
Flahavan's Revenue	30.0	32.1	+7%	Up due to higher price cup products
Flahavan's Advertising	3.5	4.5	+22%	Up to support programs
Flahavan's Promotions	1.2	1.7	+29%	Up due to new products and PR
Flahavan's Profit	5.4	5.9	+9%	

Flahavan's 2009 Marketing Plan

The Main Risk Facing the Business is Product Cost

Risks	Contingencies
1. Sharp rise in product costs —Plan anticipates a 2.5% increase —Commodity costs have been volatile	Lead a list price increase if required to achieve plan Spend back part 50% of the price increase to further support category
2. Increased promotional activity from competitors	Shift advertising creative from category building to differentiation
3. Category building efforts are unsuccessful	Develop new creative to ensure strong communication

Flahavan's 2009 Marketing Plan

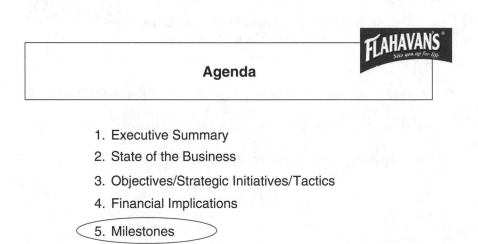

Agenda

1. Executive Summary

2. State of the Business

3. Objectives/Strategic Initiatives/Tactics

4. Financial Implications

5. Milestones

Flahavan's 2009 Marketing Plan

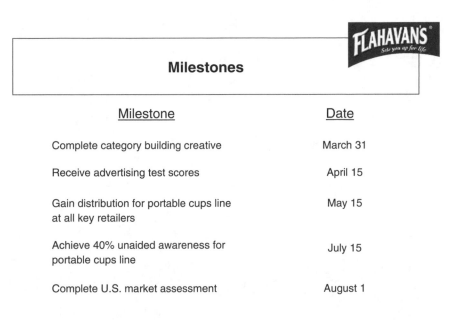

Milestones

Milestone	Date
Complete category building creative	March 31
Receive advertising test scores	April 15
Gain distribution for portable cups line at all key retailers	May 15
Achieve 40% unaided awareness for portable cups line	July 15
Complete U.S. market assessment	August 1

Flahavan's 2009 Marketing Plan

Flahavan's is Poised for Further Growth

- Flahavan's has delivered strong results, with 2008 profits up +8%, due to robust category growth and a modest price increase

- Flahavan's has two goals for 2009: increase profit by +9% and maintain share of the porridge category at 62.1%

- The 2009 marketing plan is focused on three big initiatives
  —Continue to drive category growth by promoting health benefits
  —Launch quick oats portable cups to address growing need for convenience and build margins
  —Evaluate new snacking line and expansion into U.S. market

- The primary risk facing the business is that product costs may increase more than expected. If this occurs we will increase list prices to maintain margins

Flahavan's 2009 Marketing Plan

CHAPTER 10

Twenty Strategic Initiatives

The heart of any marketing plan is the strategic initiatives; these are the big moves a business will make to achieve its objectives. This is the part of the marketing plan that really matters; it should be the focus for much of the discussion and debate.

Unfortunately, many people struggle to create tight strategic initiatives; they confuse strategic initiatives with objectives or tactics. This leads to a muddled plan.

The most important thing to remember is that objectives are what you hope to achieve with the business. In many cases the main objective will be profit. Strategic initiatives are what you will do to achieve the objective.

This chapter presents 20 different strategic initiatives. Not every one of these initiatives is appropriate for every business. More importantly, perhaps, there is no business in the world that could pursue all 20 initiatives at the same time. The goal for this chapter is to provide examples of strategic initiatives and to spark your thinking and ideas.

BUILD AWARENESS

If customers don't know about your product, they won't buy it. This is the basic reason why people worry about awareness so much, and why building it shows up in so many marketing plans.

Importantly, brand awareness on its own is not helpful; people can be aware of a brand and have no interest in buying it, and this is not a good thing. Even worse, people can have awareness of something and actively dislike it.

Tactics

The most common and obvious way to build awareness is advertising; broad-reach advertising vehicles such as television ads and print ads have an enormous impact on awareness. When a broad-reach advertising campaign kicks in on a new product, awareness will almost always shoot up.

Importantly, advertising isn't the only way to build awareness; there are literally hundreds of different tactics that will have an impact. Indeed, anything that gets your product in front of people will contribute to awareness to at least a minor degree.

Measurement

For most businesses, awareness is fairly simple to measure through surveys. It is possible to measure unaided awareness, asking questions such as, "What brands of potato chip can you think of?" It is also possible to mention aided awareness by asking questions such as "Are you aware of Wise Potato Chips?" Unaided awareness is of more value and harder to build.

EXPAND DISTRIBUTION

People won't buy a product if they can't. A product that is not in distribution has no hope of generating sales. A basic marketing task, then, is to ensure that a product or service has good distribution. For some products, this means ensuring that stores carry the product. For other products, expanding distribution means increasing the number of distributors that carry the product.

Expanding distribution on its own will not guarantee success; there has to be demand to actually drive sales. A retailer won't carry a product for very long if there isn't demand for it; retailers only make money by selling things. As a result, distribution needs to be paired with other marketing initiatives to ensure that demand is in place to drive sales once distribution increases.

Tactics

There are two important tactics to consider when expanding distribution. The first is incentives; people respond to incentives, so a strong incentive can be a powerful driver of distribution. Offering a 35 percent discount to retailers who start carrying a product, for example, is a strong incentive that could translate into results.

The second tactic to consider is expanding the sales force. Adding sales-people means you will have more people calling on channel partners, and more calls should in turn result in more distribution.

It is useful to think of distributors and retailers as customers, and market to them just as you would market to end consumers; you need to understand your channel partners just like you understand your end customers and select marketing tactics with the same amount of care. The better you know your channel partners and what motivates them, the more likely it is that you can create a compelling offer and achieve your goals.

Measurement

Distribution is easy to measure in most industries; you can simply track how many retailers or distributors carry your product, and how much they carry.

There is an important distinction between having distribution and having high-quality distribution. A retailer that carries just one item from a 20-item line has distribution, but the quality is low. As a result, marketers may want to watch absolute distribution (such as percent of retailers in a market carrying at least one item) and quality of distribution (such as average number of items carried).

BUILD BUYING RATE

Buying rate, or the average purchase rate among customers, is a critical business driver, because sales of a product are always the number of customers multiplied by the average rate of purchase. Mathematically this is always true. Increasing buying rate, then, is one important way to build a business.

Increasing buying rate is a compelling lever, because it involves selling to your existing customers, and these people are generally easy to reach and favorably inclined to your brand already.

Tactics

Buying rate tactics should spark more frequent purchase of products. One way to do this is through incentives such as frequent flyer programs, frequent buyer cards, and bulk purchase discounts; these offers reward larger and more frequent purchases with greater and greater incentives.

Buying rate tactics can also include reminder advertising, product quality improvements, and loyalty programs. The more you connect with your customers and make them feel connected to the brand, the more you can build buying rate.

An increase in buying rate can come from an increase in total category purchasing or from an increase in loyalty. These are quite different; increasing the category involves selling the overall category benefit and driving use of the entire category. Increasing loyalty is changing the mix of products purchased in a category from one brand to another.

Measurement

Buying rate can be measured in several different ways. In the best case scenario, a company has data on each customer; with this data it is possible to track purchase rate by person over time. A credit card company, for example, can watch monthly purchases to get an immediate read on buying rate at a customer level.

Surveys can also be used to evaluate buying rate, by asking customers how frequently they are buying the product. This approach is not as accurate as customer-level purchase information, but for some products this is all that is available.

BUILD PENETRATION

Penetration measures the number of customers a brand has. Since sales of a product in a given period are always the number of customers multiplied by the average purchases per customer in that period, increasing the number of customers, or building penetration, is an important and common strategic initiative. This is especially true for new or small brands.

Every product in the world has to think about attracting new customers. An existing customer base will always gradually erode as people move, companies merge and fold, and needs change. As a result, whether new or established, at some point a product has to think about attracting new people to the franchise.

Tactics

Several things must happen to build penetration: People have to be aware of the product, have access to the product, be interested in buying the product, and be motivated to do so. Each of these steps can be a strategic initiative on its own, or the basis for tactical decisions.

Penetration tactics might include broad advertising to build awareness, sampling programs to drive trial, or high-value incentives for new customers. Indeed, anything that helps convert a nonuser into a user can be considered as a penetration tactic.

Measurement

Penetration can be measured as an absolute number or as a percentage of customers in a market. Both are valid ways to look at penetration, but they do different things. Measuring as an absolute number makes it easy to link penetration to sales. However, measuring absolute numbers ignores industry trends; increasing customers by +5 percent is good but not a great accomplishment if the number of customers in the industry increased +25 percent in the same period. Measuring penetration as a percentage shows relative standing, or what percent of customers in a category buy your brand. This approach shows progress versus competition but isn't directly linked to sales; in a declining category it would be possible to increase percent penetration while the absolute number of customers declines.

One challenge in measuring penetration is that the number of customers a brand has is constantly shifting; things never stand still. Penetration is driven by two factors: the number of new customers less the number of lost customers. If there are many people giving up on a brand, the number of new customers could be substantial, but the total number of customers may not increase. As a result, the very best approach is to measure total penetration, the number of new customers, and the number of lost customers.

BUILD EXTENDED USAGE

One way to increase buying rate is to increase extended usage. This involves getting customers to do new things with a particular product. For example, people now use Arm & Hammer baking soda in all sorts of different ways; they put a box in the freezer, brush their teeth with it, and, my personal favorite, pour it down the drain. This is good for the brand, since the core use of baking soda—baking—is declining quickly in the U.S. market.

Building extended usage is appealing; it is highly incremental and not likely to prompt a competitive battle. The challenge is that it can be very difficult to do because it involves changing the way people think about a brand. Extended usage campaigns can also cause confusion; encouraging people to use margarine to moisturize their hair may lead people to wonder whether the product is really food or a beauty product. Promoting this idea could actually hurt the base business, since most people don't eat beauty products.

Tactics

Building extended use is much like launching a new product. The only difference is that the focus is on an idea instead of a specific product. For a new use to take hold, people have to be aware of the idea (awareness), be motivated to try it (trial), and then try it again (repeat).

There are different tactics for each of these steps; advertising builds awareness, for example, but is not great for driving repeat purchases. Sampling programs drive trial but are ineffective at building awareness due to their small scale.

Measurement

Extended usage ideas can be measured like any other new product; it is possible to track awareness, trial, and repeat. The best way to gather this data is surveys, asking customers about the idea. Awareness evaluates how many people have heard of the idea, on either an aided or unaided basis. Trial looks at how many people have actually tried the idea. Repeat measures the number of people who have come back to try it again.

Increase Loyalty

One way to drive sales is to increase loyalty with existing customers. Ideally, a brand has customers who are highly loyal, devoting all their purchases in a category to the brand.

Loyalty-building efforts focus on ensuring that customers don't use competitive products. For example, a consulting firm might encourage current clients to send all their projects to the firm.

Tactics

Loyalty can be built in many different ways. The key, of course, is that all efforts are aimed squarely at current consumers, the people buying the product today.

The most common loyalty efforts are incentives, or promotions that encourage customers to increase loyalty. This includes "buy two, get one free" deals and frequent buyer cards. These incentives can be very powerful; giving customers an incentive to buy a brand they are already buying will usually result in incremental sales. The problem is that these incentives can encourage customers to wait for discounts to purchase product. More importantly, incentives can erode quality perceptions.

Loyalty efforts can also include tactics such as focused advertising, relationship-building programs, and product improvements. For business-to-business companies, tactics in this area might include relationship-building and volume discounts.

Measurement

One way to quantitatively measure loyalty is share of requirements. This calculation is simply a customer's purchases from a particular company divided by the same customer's purchases of the entire category. Increasing loyalty will then translate into an increase in share of requirements.

The data behind share of requirements is readily available in some categories; it is very easy to purchase share of requirements information in many consumer products categories. In the commercial airplane market, loyalty information is well known across the industry; there is no question which airlines are flying which planes. In other categories it can be difficult to obtain loyalty information, forcing a company to rely on surveys to measure.

STRENGTHEN IN-STORE MERCHANDISING

Any product sold in a retail environment has to worry about in-store merchandising, or the type of support it is getting in store. It doesn't take a PhD in marketing to realize that if customers can't find a product in the store, they won't buy it, or that a product stacked high in the front of a store will sell a lot more than a product that can only be found on a high shelf at the back of the store.

There is a difference between having a product in distribution and getting good in-store merchandising. Getting into distribution involves establishing an initial presence. Getting good support focuses on securing a good place on shelf and then getting a prominent position in the store.

Tactics

A strong sales organization is usually essential to get good in-store support; for most products, having people physically visiting stores will help enormously, because these people can put up signs and stack up the product. Frito-Lay, for example, has salespeople visiting retailers almost every day, replenishing product and making sure that the Frito-Lay products are displayed prominently.

There are a number of other tactics that can also help with in-store merchandising, such as developing collateral materials such as signs and display units and giving retailers financial incentives.

Measurement

In-store merchandising can be easy to measure by tracking the absolute level of activity in the store. For example, it is possible to look at the number of products on the shelf, the number of secondary displays in the store, and the number of signs up.

In some categories, this information is generated by market research firms. This makes getting and tracking the data a simple process. In other categories, this information can be harder to assemble, forcing managers to rely on report from the sales force or commission a special study.

IMPROVE PRODUCT QUALITY

A very simple way to drive better business results is to improve the product. A better product will lead to happier customers, and happier customers will lead to increased sales and profits. This might come from increased loyalty, or it might come from increased use of the category in total.

The challenge in improving quality, of course, is that it generally increases product cost. Quality is rarely free. This additional cost needs to be offset somewhere else in the P&L to avoid a drop in profits.

Ultimately better product quality should result in higher sales, but this link is frequently hard to see. For a quality improvement to translate into higher sales, customers have to notice the better quality and then change purchase patterns as a result. This can take time. Telling people that the product is now "new and improved" can actually cause a sales decline; the people using a product probably already like it, and the improvement might not actually be better.

Tactics

In most cases there are obvious ways to improve quality. Reducing defects, improving reliability, adding features, and enhancing customer service are all ways to improve quality.

The challenge, of course, is figuring out which quality improvements are most valued by customers; it is impossible to do everything, so a manager has to choose which things to focus on. Market research can help with this, but only to a certain degree; market research is rarely perfect.

Any change in the product or service experience needs to reflect the brand. Improving style is not necessarily an improvement for a brand built on tradition. Strengthening health benefits is not always a good thing for a brand grounded in indulgence. Enhancing taste can be a bad thing if a brand is all about consistency, as Coca-Cola learned in the 1980s with its introduction of New Coke.

Measurement

Quality is fairly easy to measure. In fact, the challenge in measuring quality is not finding something to measure, it is figuring out which metrics are most relevant.

The options go on and on. A company can track defects, product returns, and customer complaints. A company can also evaluate overall customer satisfaction over time in a variety of ways.

The most important thing when it comes to quality is to measure something and do it consistently to see how the measure changes over time.

DECREASE PRODUCT COSTS

A powerful way to drive profits is to reduce product costs. A reduction in costs will result in a direct increase in profits, assuming sales remain relatively constant. The challenge is simply to find opportunities to reduce costs while maintaining overall customer satisfaction, or to find opportunities where the financial benefit of a cost reduction outweighs the volume impact.

Tactics

There are dozens of ways to reduce costs on a business. A company can increase line efficiency, utilize cheaper materials, negotiate lower prices on key raw materials, reformulate to cut product costs, or eliminate costly and unnecessary features.

The challenge, of course, is to ensure that the cost-saving moves do not reduce sales or hurt the brand. This can be hard to determine; will customers notice if the label has two colors instead of three? Will anyone care if the product comes in a thinner package?

There is a great temptation to pursue cost-saving opportunities that hurt product quality and customer satisfaction. The benefits of such a move are immediate, certain, and quantifiable. The costs of such a move, decreased brand equity and ultimately lower sales, are in the future, uncertain, and hard to quantify. As a result, smart people can make very poor decisions when it comes to cost-savings projects, reducing quality despite the obvious risk.

Measurement

Measuring cost-saving initiatives is fairly easy; it is simply the process of tracking each program and identifying the amount saved.

It is far more difficult to evaluate the impact of the cost-saving move on quality and customer satisfaction; these changes are often subtle and hard to see. Will anyone notice if there is a little less ketchup on a hamburger? Even if they notice, will anyone care? Although the answer to both questions may be no, a series of small moves such as this can result in low quality products and weak brands. Proceed with caution!

Introduce a New Brand

Launching a new brand is one of the biggest investments a company can make; the cost of gaining distribution, creating awareness, building trial, and securing repeat is substantial. Creating a new brand is also an incredibly powerful way to drive growth. It is a high-risk and high-reward proposition.

In almost all cases, a new brand should have its own marketing plan, highlighting how it will succeed in the market and laying out priorities for the launch. However, a new brand will almost always be a strategic initiative in a broader marketing plan. At the finest level, the new brand will have its own marketing plan. For the business unit, however, it might simply be a strategic initiative.

Tactics

Many things go into successfully launching a new brand; the topic warrants a book on its own. It is important to remember, however, that four things are essential if a new brand is to succeed. First, the brand needs to gain awareness; people have to know it exists. Second, the brand has to secure distribution; customers have to have access to it. Third, the brand has to gain trial. Fourth, people have to come back and purchase the brand's product again. Each of these tasks needs dedicated tactics.

Measurement

The success of a new brand is fairly simple to measure by tracking revenue or sales; this is the number that matters most during a launch. Ultimately, profit will matter most, of course, but during the launch, sales are a better indicator; without sales there of course will be no profits.

Revenue doesn't say much about why a new brand is succeeding or not. Revenue is simply the result. As a result, it is important to measure other things, such as awareness, distribution, and trial. These things do not on their own matter, but they are important diagnostics for understanding how well the new product is doing.

Attract Competitors' Customers

One sure way to build a business is to steal your competitors' customers. Most markets are, to some degree, zero-sum games; the more you grow, the more your competition loses and vice versa. As a result, directly targeting your competition can be a powerful way to build a business.

Tactics

Tactics that attract your competition's customers fall into two big areas: incentives and messages. Incentives include all the different offers and promotions you can use to bring in your competition's customers. For example, a bank may offer a substantial cash payment for new customers who open a direct-deposit checking account; these people are probably just switching from another bank. Similarly, a credit card may offer zero percent interest for new customers. Again, this offer is for people switching from the competition.

Messages include all the things a company can say about a product or service to get someone to switch. This might include highlighting unique features in the product or service, or direct product comparisons. One of the most famous examples of this is the Pepsi Challenge, a head-to-head product comparison of Coke and Pepsi.

Targeting is critical when it comes to going after your competitors' customers; you want to focus your message exclusively on that group. In many cases, you do not want to reach your current customers with the same effort; a high-value trial promotion might be effective at getting your competition's customers to purchase your product, but you don't want to give your current customers the same offer, or even let them know you are offering it to other people.

The risk in targeting your competition's customers is that you can quickly get into a competitive battle; each company offers big incentives for people to switch and attacks other products in the category. This can lead to lots of inefficient switching and damage the entire category.

Measurement

It can be difficult to measure this strategic initiative for two reasons. First, it is often hard to identify how many new customers are coming in to the franchise. Second, it often isn't clear where a new customer comes from: is it someone new to the category, or someone switching from the competition?

Nonetheless, it is important to measure something. If it isn't possible to identify actual customers coming from the competition, the focus should shift to total customer count (also called penetration) and overall sales.

DEFEND AGAINST A NEW COMPETITIVE PRODUCT

A company with a strong position in an attractive market needs to aggressively defend its position. In many cases, there will be a steady stream of competitive attacks, as different companies attempt to get a piece of the action. Ensuring that the challengers fail to establish a place in the market is a critically important task. Any time a meaningful new competitor shows up, a company should mount a defensive effort.

Tactics

The goal in most defensive efforts is clear: kill the attacker. This isn't pleasant work; it is tough and brutal. Companies don't like to discuss defensive efforts for obvious reasons; there is a fine line between a tough fight and illegal anticompetitive behavior.

When considering defensive programs, it is useful to remember that every business has to make money; this is the goal of essentially every for-profit organization in the world. As a result, the mission of a defender is to convince the attacker that it will be impossible to make money with the new initiative. If a defender can blow up the attacker's financial proposition, the attacker will stop. People don't do things to lose money.

A defensive effort needs to consider timing. Every new product has to do four things: gain distribution, build awareness, build trial, and secure repeat. These are basically sequential, as one step leads to the next. A company can defend at each step. Tactics vary depending on timing; trade incentives may be an effective way to block distribution, but it will do little to impact repeat. Loading programs are powerful tools for limiting trial but won't have a big impact on awareness.

Measurement

Defensive efforts can be hard to measure, because the objective is to impact someone else's results. Still, it is usually possible to get at least some indication of how the attacker is doing. A defensive goal might be limiting the attacker to a certain share of a category or a certain amount of revenue, or it could even be the demise of the competitive product entirely.

Enter a New Market

Entering a new market is an obvious way to build a business. If you expand into a new city, region, or country, you will attract new customers and build sales and profits. This is the theory, at least. The reality is often challenging indeed.

Tactics

Entering a new market is very much like launching a new product. Indeed, in the new area, your product really is just another new business, trying to break into a new market.

As a result, the same four new product steps apply: gain distribution, build awareness, get trial, and secure repeat. Each of these steps requires effort and thought, and there are different tactics to drive each one. Building distribution requires a sales organization and incentives. Gaining awareness depends on advertising and public relations efforts. Trial depends on sampling and incentives. Repeat depends on incentives and reminders.

Measurement

The success of a launch in a new geography is easy to determine by monitoring sales and market share versus plan.

As with any new product, it is wise to supplement sales with other measures, because sales looks at the total impact; it is not diagnostic. There are other measures that can help diagnose what is working and not: it is possible to measure distribution, awareness, trial, and repeat.

INCREASE REFERRALS

Referrals can be essential for a business; in some categories, referrals play a critically important role in driving trial. Dentists, for example, depend heavily on referrals for new patients. Consultants, accountants, financial planners, and churches are all businesses where referrals are a key lever.

Increasing referrals is a logical strategic initiative for many businesses; for a dentist, an increase in referrals will directly lead to an increase in new patients. It could also lead to an increase in loyalty among people doing the referring—people who refer are often the most loyal.

Tactics

Referrals can be hard to impact. It is possible to build awareness of a brand simply by buying a lot of advertising and getting in front of people. Similarly, it is possible to build trial with very heavy incentives aimed at new customers. Referrals, however, are harder to impact because they are largely out of the control of the organization.

It is possible, however, to encourage referrals through different marketing moves. Incentives such as a discount if someone refers to a friend can certainly motivate someone, though this incentive may reduce the impact of the referral somewhat. It is better to simply ask customers: "So who else might need this service?" or "Will you recommend me to your colleagues?" Pharmaceutical giant Merck aggressively sought referrals during the 2007 launch of its vaccine Gardasil, running ads asking people to "Tell Someone."

MEASUREMENT

Referrals can be difficult to measure; it is very hard to understand how often your brand is being referred to other people. However, there are ways to evaluate the success of a referral campaign.

One way to measure this is to look at the number of new customers. Since referrals should lead to new customers, it is possible to track the number of new customers to see if it is increasing following the launch of a referral campaign.

More directly, you can ask new customers how they heard about the brand or the company, and note what share of new customers mention a referral.

REPOSITION THE BRAND

Repositioning a brand is a classic strategic initiative. Brands are not always a positive; brands can be negative, neutral, or positive. As a result, there are times when it is necessary to deliberately change what a brand means. A brand that stands for cheap and low quality may find this is a difficult set of associations to work with. A brand that seems old may well fail to attract younger people.

If a brand has a negative image, or a negative set of associations that is hurting the business, there are only two viable options. The first option is to change the associations, or reposition the brand. The second option is to give up on the brand entirely. The second option is, for obvious reasons, not appealing.

Not every repositioning will succeed, because it can be very difficult to change the associations around a well-known and established brand. Getting people to think of Wal-Mart as a place to buy fashionable products will be difficult. General Motors has been trying to reposition its Cadillac brand for many years, with somewhat limited success. Similarly, it will be a long time until people see Iraq as peaceful, prosperous nation.

Still, given the alternatives, repositioning can be a critical strategic initiative for a business with a weak brand.

Tactics

The challenge in repositioning a brand is that existing customers may leave faster than new customers arrive. Any time the associations around a brand change, some customers will leave; they liked the old brand better than the new brand. This is inevitable. The challenge is that if the existing customers leave all at once, the financial results on a brand can deteriorate quickly. But attracting new people to a brand takes time. People won't rush to a brand simply because the packaging and the advertising changed; it takes time to earn credibility. As a result, a brand going through a repositioning may well lose sales at such a pace that the business begins to implode. This is a substantial risk.

Virtually everything that a business does has an impact on the brand, which means almost every tactic can be deployed in a repositioning. All of the 4 Ps (product, place, price, promotion) are up for discussion. The greater the repositioning, the more things will need to change.

Advertising is usually a large part of a brand repositioning effort, because advertising is a uniquely broad-reach vehicle. Few things can match the impact of a well-crafted television campaign. Public relations efforts can play a major role, too, as can endorsements, partnerships, pricing, and packaging. Indeed, virtually any marketing tactic can be deployed to support a repositioning.

MEASUREMENT

It can be a challenge to track the success of a brand repositioning effort for the very simple reason that sales are generally a poor measure. Indeed, during a repositioning, sales frequently decline; current customers may depart quickly while new customers are slow to appear. A sales decline may suggest that the repositioning is not working when the reverse is actually true. Worst case, a repositioning that is going well may appear to be a failure, leading the company to declare the repositioning a flop and reverse course.

The best measures to evaluate a brand repositioning are those that look at the imagery of a brand and composition of the brand franchise. For example, a change in the associations around a brand could be a major indicator of success for a repositioning. Similarly, a change in the group of people buying a brand might indicate success; for a brand attempting to attract a younger consumer base, a drop in the average age of the franchise would be a step forward.

It is essential to set modest targets for a repositioning because it takes time and effort. Repositioning efforts do not yield fruit quickly.

ENTER A NEW DISTRIBUTION CHANNEL

Entering a new distribution channel can be a very effective way to drive incremental sales and reach new customers. Tractor maker John Deere, for example, relied exclusively on its own dealers for many years. In 2005, however, the company started selling through mass retailers such as Home Depot. This move built sales and broadened the customer base, because John Deere tractors were now readily available to a much larger group of people.

Changes in a distribution system are major moves, because they usually have a long-term impact. In addition, these moves can increase sales substantially. They can also create conflict between channels and bring about long-term complexity. In addition, a distribution channel decision can have a major impact on the brand, for better or for worse. The challenge is to evaluate the potential for incremental gain versus the increased risk of conflict and confusion and damage to the brand.

Tactics

Entering a new channel is a major undertaking; it requires focus and determination. In most cases, tactics supporting the expansion include an expanded sales effort and promotional incentives. However, the expansion may also require a broader marketing effort to inform consumers of the change, including advertising and online marketing.

It is important to focus on existing channels, too, during the expansion to new channels; declines in the existing channel can easily overwhelm any gains from the new channel.

Measurement

Progress in the new channel is easy to measure, because sales volume is a simple and clear indicator of success. By setting a clear sales target, it is easy to see how things are going with the new initiative. More defined measures, such as level of distribution and sales velocity, can also help monitor success and diagnose precisely what is happening.

It is more difficult to measure how the distribution change is affecting the entire franchise. Cannibalization can be hard to see. For example; are declines in the existing channel due to people moving to the new channel? Or is the existing channel not executing well? Or is the category simply declining overall?

As a result, it is important to establish measures for the existing channel. In particular, it is essential to gather customer-level information through customer surveys, so that you can evaluate how growth in one channel is impacting the other.

INCREASE PRICING

Increasing prices is perhaps the world's most perfect marketing move. It is simple, quick, certain, and quantifiable. It requires no capital investment, no R&D work, and no creative development.

More importantly, it can have a dramatic impact on a business. If a business has a bottom-line margin of 5 percent, then a tiny +1 percent increase in price will increase profits by +20 percent, less the impact of sales declines.

There are problems with price increases, of course. In almost all cases, a price increase will result in lower sales, and for some businesses, the gains from a price increase can be overwhelmed by the resulting losses in volume, so the price increase ends up increasing profits only slightly, or actually decreases profits. The key question is price elasticity. A business with very high price elasticity will find it difficult to justify a price increase, because sales volumes will fall off substantially as prices go up. A business with low price elasticity will profit handsomely from an increase in price because sales will fall only slightly with a price increase.

This is why it is so important to have differentiation on a business. Businesses that are highly differentiated and preferred by customers generally have lower price elasticity. Businesses that lack differentiation have high price elasticity.

Tactics

Increasing prices is usually a very simple matter: just increase prices. This is one of the reasons pricing is such a wonderful tactic. It's about as simple as it gets.

However, it is important to keep in mind several factors when raising prices. First, timing can be important: when should you announce a price increase? When is it effective? Generally, customers will stock up if they know a price increase is coming. This will lead to a sharp increase in sales, followed by a decline as customers work down their inventory. This volume swing can create operational issues and financial issues, and so it is important to manage the size of the buyout by reducing the time customers have to buy at the old price and capping the amount customers can purchase at the old price.

Second, channel issues may make pricing difficult. Many companies sell to distributors or retailers, not to the end customer. In this case, it is important to think through how the price increase will be received. Will distributors push back? Will they use the price increase as a change to increase their prices, too? Understanding how distribution partners will react to the price increase is essential to ensure success.

Third, it is critical to think about how competitors will react to the price increase. You can't talk to your competitors about pricing; this is generally illegal and unethical. However, it is important to think about how they will react to the price increase. Will they follow your price increase, or not? What usually happens in the market? Being aware of the category norms and pricing history is important, to ensure your pricing move is optimal from a competitive perspective.

Measurement

For most businesses, pricing is easy to see. Indeed, it isn't even necessary to evaluate whether or not the price increase is in place: if prices are up then, well, prices are up.

In some cases pricing is not quite so obvious. If a sales force has the ability to negotiate prices, then ensuring that prices actually go up requires evaluation, and monitoring this becomes important.

There are several things to watch and measure, however, as the price increase flows into the market. First, it is critical to watch competition. Did your competitors match the pricing move? Any price move should have assumptions about likely competitive response. Once the price increase is in place, it is possible to then see if competition is acting as expected.

Second, if you sell through a distributor or retailer, it is important to evaluate their response. Did they pass on the price increase? Are prices to end customers going up? Is the increase more than you expected, or less?

Third, it is critical to watch how pricing is affecting sales. Seeing this, however, can be difficult; sales on a business are driven by many things, so identifying precisely the impact of the price increase can be hard. However, it is generally possible to see major shifts, such as a major and abrupt drop in sales.

Strengthen the Brand

Building a brand is a key marketing task; for many companies brands are the most important assets. A common and important marketing initiative is strengthening the brand, ensuring that the brand is strong and preferred by customers. Brand loyalty is both powerful and enduring.

Tactics

Every point of contact a person has with a brand shapes the associations. So while advertising certainly has a major impact on a brand, a marketer needs to also consider customer service, public relations, and every other place customers see or interact with the brand.

There are many, many tactics that can build a brand. Advertising, customer service, promotional offers, logos, slogans, and public relations efforts all impact the brand. Brand building efforts should be based in an understanding of the customer and the brand. Once you know how customers feel about your brand, it is possible to develop tactics that can strengthen the relationship.

For example, if customers know your brand and like your brand, but don't see it as different from competition, it would be natural to highlight points of difference through communication vehicles. If customers understand your brand but don't feel particularly connected to it, you could create ways for people to become more involved in the brand, through events and other engaging activities.

Measurement

Measuring the strength of a brand can be a challenge. A brand is a set of associations linked to a name, mark, or symbol. The challenge in measurement is to evaluate the strength and nature of these associations and, in particular, see how they change as your marketing effort unfolds.

The best way to measure a brand is through quantitative techniques such as consumer surveys that ask about brand awareness, brand perceptions, and brand purchase intent.

It can be very hard to see the impact of a marketing campaign aimed at strengthening associations, because well-established brands change very slowly. As a result, the changes can sometimes be impossible to see in a quantitative survey; the margin of error in the survey may obscure the impact of the campaign. This doesn't necessarily mean the campaign is not working. Setting modest goals is important in a campaign to strengthen the brand. Indeed, it is best to monitor the tactics, such as attendance at events or visits to a Web site, in addition to the core brand equity measures.

Test New Marketing Tactics

The best way to learn about new marketing tactics is to try them. Simply talking about potential ideas is insufficient. Until you actually try something, you won't know for sure whether the tactic will work for your business. As a result, testing is critical; you have to try new things.

Any business leader responsible for delivering financial results faces a very simple problem. Old marketing tactics may not work particularly well, but they are generally predictable and certain. If you rely on the proven levers, chances are good that you will reach your goals. It might not be optimal, but you will probably get there. New marketing tactics might be much better than the old tactics, but the new tactics are uncertain and unproven. They might be better, but then again they might be worse. If you bet on the new tactics you might be a hero, but you also might be a dog; there is a very good chance you will miss your plan, and that is an unappealing proposition.

The tension between the old, predictable tactics and the new, unproven tactics explains why many new marketing techniques catch on so slowly. Why take the risk?

For prudent marketers, the only way to embrace new things is to try them in a modest way while maintaining the proven tactics. If the new tactics prove to be effective, then a more dramatic shift in spending will be both safe and effective.

Tactics

Every day, it seems, there are more ways to promote and market a product. You now can put stickers on bananas, videos on the Internet, and holographs in a train station. The options go on and on. Most of them are interesting, cool, and appealing.

The challenge is that it is impossible to test all of the new tactics; there are simply too many. In addition, each test takes time and money, both of which are limited.

The first step in experimenting with new tactics is to identify the most attractive options; it is possible to sift through the options and identify which tactics are even remotely feasible for your brand. Usually there are three things to consider. First, is the tactic scalable? In other words, will the tactic ever be big enough to matter? Some tactics are so small that in the end they will never have enough of an impact to really matter. Second, does it fit with your brand? Some tactics are simply inconsistent with a brand. An ad posted above a urinal is not the best place for Tiffany or McKinsey to be advertising. Third, do the economics make any sense? If there is no possible way a marketing tactic would be a smart financial decision, there is no reason to try it.

Once the tactics have been narrowed down, it is possible to identify the options with the greatest potential and move those into testing.

Measurement

The most important thing to remember when evaluating new marketing tactics is that the metrics must be clear before you field the test. It is very hard to figure out after the fact whether a marketing program was a success if you didn't establish the measures ahead of time. What is success, anyway?

For any marketing test, then, creating clear metrics is essential. The best measure, of course, is sales. How did the new tactic impact revenue and profit? Getting this information is easier said than done, however, so very often you will need to have a secondary measure, such as phone calls or hits to a Web site. Importantly, though, you have to have something you can measure and track and use to determine whether the tactic is successful or not.

ACCELERATE NEW PRODUCT DEVELOPMENT

New products don't just fall out of the sky. Creating a new product takes time, energy, and focus. As a result, if new product development is important for a business, it may well show up as a strategic initiative in the marketing plan. This initiative is more about creating products than actually putting them into market; accelerating new product development will, with luck, lead to new product launches in later years. If new products are an important part of the long-term plan, however, ramping up new product development is an important strategic initiative. If you don't get to work, the new products will never appear.

Tactics

Although new product development requires a mix of art and science, it is very possible to take concrete steps to accelerate the process. These steps range from establishing a cross-functional team, to hiring people with the necessary product development skills, to providing resources and fielding concept and product tests.

Putting a formal new product development process into place is an important action step. The most common new product development process involves stages and gates. Before an idea can move from one stage to the next, it has to make it through a particular gate. Therefore, before an idea can move from the concept development stage to the feasibility stage, for example, it has to have positive concept test results. Moreover, before a product can move from the feasibility stage into the product development stage, the basic financial proposition has to work.

Measurement

Evaluating the success of a new product development process is fairly easy if there is a formal process in place; it is possible to track the number of ideas at the different stages of the development process. For example, an organization could set a goal of having three different ideas make it to the product development stage by a certain time. It then becomes very easy to assess whether the new products process is on track or behind.

Similarly, simply putting the product development process into place could be a key milestone.

* * *

There is no one strategic initiative that is right for every business. Every business has unique challenges at a given point in time, and what works for one business may well not work for another. That is what makes building a business so challenging. The key is to be aware of the wide range of options available, and to use the marketing planning process to identify the initiatives that have the best chance of driving your business forward.

CHAPTER 11

Common Questions

Any discussion of marketing plans inevitably leads to questions. The ideas in this book represent an enormous shift in how many people and companies approach marketing plans, and any new idea sparks questions. What follows are the most common questions I receive when talking with people about creating breakthrough marketing plans.

How Long Should a Marketing Plan Be?

There are two easy and somewhat unsatisfying answers to this question. The first is the old favorite: it depends. The second is equally unsatisfying but more truthful: a marketing plan should be just as long as it needs to be to communicate the goals and objectives, strategic initiatives, and key tactics (GOST) and to provide compelling support. If you can do this in 20 pages, fine. If it takes you 30 pages, fine. If you can pull it off in four really good pages, even better.

The most important thing to remember is that a marketing plan should not go on and on and on. If you find yourself creating a 100-page document, immediately stop, step back, and think about what really matters. In many cases, you'll find the plan is full of information that simply isn't relevant or important. If that is the case, drop the unnecessary information and get to the point. At the very least, move the unnecessary information to the appendix.

In almost all cases, a shorter marketing plan is better than a longer marketing plan. Short plans force you to focus. It is difficult to get too confused or cluttered in a short plan; there simply isn't room. Short plans are also easy to produce, so you and your team can focus on analysis and thinking instead of document production. Simply typing, printing, and copying a 150-page marketing plan takes a lot of time. The document production process can overwhelm the meat: "We don't have time to think, we have to start printing!" is a common refrain. The lament of one executive is typical: "I think we do too little work thinking about what will drive the business, and too much time writing decks."

Most importantly, short plans are easy to understand. Since the goal of a marketing plan is to communicate a recommendation and gain support, a simple plan is more likely to be understood and to work. As Adobe's Mark Delman observed, "It has to be short. Length allows people to be sloppy. Brevity forces clarity."

Speaking coach Steve Adubato highlights the problem with long presentations. When asked about a 111-slide presentation, he observed, "That's not content. That is laziness. What that is saying is, 'If I dump a ton of information on you, I am going to make it look like I did my homework.' Well, you want to know what? Your board is not going to be impressed. They are going to be terribly bored. I think we confuse volume—quantity of information—with making a real connection."[1]

Indeed, after a certain point, each additional page detracts from the whole; it diminishes the focus, waters down the story, and increases the chance that your audience will get distracted. Marketer and investor Andy Whitman notes that length is sometimes a sign of weak thinking. He explains, "If it takes you 80 pages to cover something, I wonder if there are any ideas in there."

How Often Should a Business Write a Marketing Plan?

Most companies create marketing plans once a year, as part of an annual process of setting direction for the business. This is a reasonable approach. Over the course of the year a lot happens in a market, so taking a fresh look at the business and marketing plan every year only makes sense.

A better guideline is this: a business should write a marketing plan as often as needed to stay on track. In many cases, this means an annual plan is sufficient. In some cases, however, the business will need to update the plan far more frequently. Anytime the situation facing a business changes substantially, a new marketing plan is in order.

If a business is doing far better than expected, for example, a new marketing plan should be created to determine how the momentum can be sustained and evaluate the implications on the full year financials. If a business is struggling, a new marketing plan is needed to get things moving in the right direction. If a competitor makes a major and unexpected move, a new plan is essential to respond to the competitor's move. Similarly, if there is a major shift in a market, such as a major increase in the price of a key raw material, a new plan should be created. Indeed, in an extreme case, a business might need to create a new marketing plan every month.

The need for frequent updates is one reason why shorter plans are better; it is virtually impossible to rapidly update a 200-page plan. It is very possible to update an 11-page plan.

Although adjusting to changing conditions is essential, a business should not make major strategic changes frequently. Every strategic shift entails cost in terms of resources, time, and energy; changing course can be exceptionally costly for a business and draining for employees. A series of major strategic shifts can leave a business in chaos. Still, sticking with a plan when the situation has changed significantly makes little sense.

Most importantly, the foundation of a business should change very infrequently, if at all. Brand positioning, for example, should remain consistent year after year; the positioning provides continuity for the brand as the marketing plan changes. A brand that stands for luxury shouldn't embrace a value positioning simply because short-term business results are weak. A brand that stands for top traditional quality for one day, value the next day, and trendy style the next day will quickly come to stand for nothing at all.

How Should a Global Brand Approach Marketing Plans?

Global brands are a challenge to manage. The problem is simple: every market has unique challenges and opportunities. What works in one country may well not work in the next, and a program that builds sales in one place might actually cause a sales decline in another place.

As a result, a brand needs a different marketing plan in every market. A good marketing plan takes into account the unique dynamics facing a business. Since these dynamics change, the marketing plan needs to change. Executing the same marketing plan in Germany and Thailand is not a good idea; the markets are very different.

The problem is that brands should ideally be consistent from market to market. A brand shouldn't mean one thing in Mexico and a different thing in Brazil; this makes life very complicated and can confuse customers.

The way to ensure that a global brand feels like the same brand all around the world is to be certain that all the marketing plans are built on the same foundation. In every country, for example, the positioning of a brand should be basically the same. A consistent foundation ensures that each marketing plan will support the global brand. The strategic initiatives may be different, and the tactics will almost always be different, but the feel of the brand will be the same.

Should a Marketing Plan be Written for a Product or a Company?

A company should have a marketing plan and a product should have a marketing plan. They should be related, of course, but they are written at very different levels.

One extreme is the marketing plan written for a company. This plan outlines how the total company will compete and grow. It is generally created by the chief executive officer (CEO) and the senior management team. At Procter & Gamble (P&G), for example, A.G. Lafley will create a marketing plan for the entire corporation, highlighting the corporate objectives and the corporation's key strategic initiatives.

The other extreme is a product marketing plan. This plan lays out how a particular product will compete and achieve its objectives. The objectives are developed at a product level, with strategic initiatives appropriate for the product.

Bigger businesses, of course, have bigger and broader strategic initiatives. At the corporate level, a strategic initiative might be something like, "Grow volume in emerging markets." At a product level, a strategic initiative could be, "Win the key holiday week in store." At both levels, however, the strategic initiatives clearly convey action and direction.

Marketing plans within a larger company form a pyramid. Product level plans are the finest level plans. Category marketing plans bring together several product level plans. Division level plans span several categories. The total company marketing plan builds off the division level plans (see exhibit 11.1). At each level, the most important initiatives are highlighted. Improving product quality on a particular product might be a strategic initiative for that product, but not a big enough strategic initiative to be one of the key priorities for the division or the company.

What Happened to the Situation Analysis?

It is essential to understand the situation facing a brand, but the situation analysis shouldn't be in the marketing plan. Indeed, one reason why so many

Exhibit 11.1 Marketing Plan Pyramid

marketing plans are a waste of time is that the situation analysis takes over the entire document.

The theory behind the situation analysis is sound. Understanding the situation is important because you can't make decisions unless you first understand what is going on. Great marketing should be grounded in a deep understanding of the business, the brand, the competition, and the customer. So theoretically, a situation analysis is a very good thing.

The problem is that people very often confuse the situation analysis with the actual meat of the marketing plan. Instead of discussing the actual recommendation, the marketing plan turns into a vast research report, in which every piece of the business is analyzed at great length.

As a result, including a situation analysis in a marketing plan is simply asking for trouble, because there is a very good chance the situation analysis will grow and grow until it overwhelms the plan.

The reason to write a marketing plan in the first place is to lay out a plan, gain support, and communicate with the broader organization. The typical situation analysis doesn't help with any of these things; it is just a collection of facts and figures.

Of course, it is possible to write a tight, simple, and focused situation analysis that leads logically to the final recommendation. Done well, this approach can certainly be effective. The problem is that it is very difficult to do so; most people will get so lost in the situation analysis that the story of the business will never emerge.

This doesn't mean that a marketing manager shouldn't analyze a business. On the contrary, to develop a great marketing plan the manager needs to understand a business exceptionally well. Someone responsible for formulating a marketing plan should look at and analyze all the information that would otherwise be in the situation analysis. All the analyses, however, don't go in the plan.

A marketing plan needs some set up, but this is simply a description of how the business is doing and the challenges ahead.

What If My Boss Wants to See a Long, Traditional Marketing Plan?

Never forget that marketing plans are written for a purpose. In most cases, one important reason to create a plan is to get support. As a result, you need to keep your audience in mind; you want your plan to be well received to maximize the chances it will be approved. So it only makes sense to make the plan as appealing as you can for your audience. This is Marketing 101: delight the customer.

For example, if your decision maker likes presentations, then do a presentation. If your decision maker likes to read documents, write a document. If they like everything on purple paper, put it on purple paper. The format doesn't really matter; the ideas and substance matter.

That said, do not rush out and create a long, traditional marketing plan simply because you think that is what people want to see. It is worth clarifying the expectations. In most cases, what people really care about are the recommendations and the support.

If the request is really for a long, traditional plan, I would focus on creating a tight, focused plan followed by a detailed appendix. I suspect you will never get to the detailed section and eventually you will be able to drop it entirely.

A particularly principled person might argue that, no, if a short plan is best, then a short plan should be created, regardless of the wishes of the audience. This is intellectually brave but practically foolish. My advice is to stand on principle and take a risk when the stakes are high. Taking a huge political risk on a marketing plan doesn't make a lot of sense. Providing a short plan followed by a longer appendix is a reasonable compromise.

Shouldn't the Customer Drive the Marketing Plan?

Customers are important. Indeed, it's hard to argue that customers aren't the most important aspect of any business; if you don't have customers, you don't have a business. Delighting customers is a very good way to build a business.

However, customers should not drive the marketing plan. The goal of a business is not just to give customers what they want. The goal is to build long-term profitability. Giving customers what they want is an important way to achieve the goal, but it isn't a goal in and of itself.

In truth, delighting customers and building a great business are different things. Ideally, a business is able to do both: create happy customers and generate profits in the process. This is the ideal situation.

But it is very possible to delight customers and destroy a business in the process. For example, customers almost always want more features and lower prices; cutting prices while adding more features, however, is rarely a way to build profits over time.

As a result, while it is essential to understand customers to create a great plan, the plan cannot be all about the customer. Businesses need to think about how they can profitably meet and shape customer needs to provide value versus the competition. Jeff Immelt, CEO of General Electric, explained the situation well in a recent interview. He noted, "I've spent my lifetime working with customers, and I love customers. I get great insights from them—but I would never let them set our strategy for us. But by talking to them, I can put it in my own language. Customers always pay our bills. But they will never pick our people or set our strategies."[2]

Who Should Write the Marketing Plan?

Marketing plans should be written by the people responsible for actually implementing the plan and delivering the results. This means that a marketing plan should generally be presented and owned by whoever is responsible for the results on a business.

Curiously, this means that the marketing department should not always be responsible for creating the marketing plan. In some organizations, the marketing department is primarily focused on communications; the marketing team develops the sales materials and the advertising, but isn't responsible for the overall business performance and has limited impact on pricing decisions, product decisions, and research decisions. In this case, the marketing team should have input on the plan, but should not ultimately create it and own it. Instead, the marketing plan should be created by the general manager who owns the overall plan results.

A good marketing plan focuses on all parts of the business, not just the communications. As a result, the marketing plan should be created by the people who are responsible for all part of the business. In some cases the general manager is a marketing executive. In other cases, the general manager has a background in sales, operations, or finance. In every case, however, the general manager has to understand and believe in the plan. The person on the hook for delivering the profit numbers will ultimately call the shots on the business.

Marketing plans also should be written by relatively senior people, the individuals who know a business well and can think through the best plan. Since the marketing plan plays a critical role in the long-term success of a business, it requires the attention of senior executives. Delegating the plan to a junior person, or an outside agency, is a recipe for trouble.

But this is exactly what happens at many companies. Very often, the people least capable of developing powerful strategies—the junior people—are the ones charged with developing them. Eli Lilly's Michael McGrath notes that at many companies, the person creating the marketing plan "...tends to be the associate right out of business school, because no one else wants to do it." This is not a wise approach.

What Role Should the Chief Marketing Officer Plan?

The chief marketing officer (CMO) should be deeply involved in creating marketing plans. Indeed, one of the primary tools a CMO can use to foster a marketing mindset in a company is to champion and support a marketing planning process; this elevates the discussion of marketing and gets people focused on how the marketing can build the business.

However, the CMO should not actually create and write the plan unless he or she is the general manager and owns the P&L. Having the CMO write the plan seems like an obvious decision, because the CMO is head of, well, marketing. However, the CMO is often the wrong person to write the plan, because frequently the CMO doesn't have responsibility for the business results. In many companies, the CMO plays a functional role, reporting to the CEO, and serving as a marketing advisor across the company. In this situation, the CMO should not create the marketing plan, because the CMO doesn't own the P&L.

Without ownership of the P&L, the CMO can establish the process, set the standards, and review and comment on the plans. But the CMO should not develop and own the plan; the plan always has to come from the person or team ultimately responsible for the business results. At P&G, for example, Chief Marketing Officer Jim Stengel has no direct profit responsibility; the people responsible for delivering the profit numbers work in the operating divisions. In this case, Stengel should not be developing marketing plans. He is not accountable for the results, so he should not be writing the plan. The marketing plans should be created by the business teams. The CMO should have input into the plans, certainly, but ultimately the plan is the responsibility of the team responsible for driving the overall business results.

SHOULDN'T EVERY MARKETING PLAN INCLUDE A SWOT ANALYSIS?

A SWOT analysis is not a required part of a marketing plan, and most marketing plans would be better without it. A SWOT analysis is a useful tool for analyzing a business; it is always good to understand an organization's strengths, weaknesses, opportunities, and threats. Laying these things out in an organized fashion makes very good sense. Indeed, the SWOT analysis is a useful tool for learning about a business and the situation ahead.

However, a SWOT analysis should generally not be part of a final marketing plan; it can help shape a plan, but it should rarely appear in the final document.

SWOT analyses have several problems that make them more appropriate for analysis than the actual plan. First, a SWOT analysis simply reviews the situation as it exists; the analysis organizes existing data. The analysis doesn't say anything about what should be done; the implications are often not obvious and the link to the ensuing plan is tenuous at best. A SWOT analysis certainly isn't a plan. It is also a weak tool for supporting a plan; the information in a SWOT analysis can generally be presented in a far more powerful manner, as part of a broader story.

As AspireUp's Roland Jacobs explained, "The SWOT analysis is just a repository of thoughts about the business." Another marketing executive was even more direct when discussing the SWOT, noting, "If I see a SWOT analysis in a marketing plan, I am actually more nervous that they have no plan."

In short, a SWOT analysis is a fine analytic tool for organizing information, but it should generally not be part of a marketing plan.

DOES AN ORGANIZATION NEED A MARKETING PLANNING PROCESS?

Every organization should develop marketing plans and every organization needs a marketing plan process. Marketing plans don't create themselves.

Without a process for creating, reviewing, and monitoring plans, few people will actually create a plan. There needs to be deliverables and deadlines.

Some organizations have incredibly long and detailed marketing planning processes. For example, the marketing plan process at one company I worked with required six pages to summarize. The process kicked off every year in January and ended with approved plans in November. It was a complicated, elaborate, global affair.

However, a marketing plan process doesn't need to be long, complex, and drawn out. Although some organizations will inevitably end up with a complicated system simply because the organization is enormous and complicated, this is not a given. A marketing plan process can be very simple.

Whether simple or complex, every organization needs to have something: a logical process and timeline for creating a plan. Otherwise nothing will happen.

Ideally the marketing plan process is created and owned by the senior management team. Ideally, the CEO or chief operating officer (COO) should be deeply involved in the process. Marketing is essential for business success, so a CEO or COO ultimately should drive and own the process.

If senior management isn't engaged in the planning process, it is up to the business leaders or marketing leaders to champion the cause. If a process doesn't exist, it is up to marketing leaders to create one.

What Does a Good Planning Process Look Like?

Great marketing plan processes have several common characteristics; these hold true whether process is short or long, simple or complicated, focused or thorough.

First, the process must be cross-functional. A marketing plan that only includes the marketing department will fail to have a big impact on an organization. Marketing plans are by nature cross-functional; marketing touches R&D, sales, operations, finance, and sometimes even human resources. A marketing plan that is created solely by marketers will lack cross-functional support and will not incorporate cross-functional considerations.

A marketing plan is different from an operations plan; marketing is not simply another function. Marketing touches everything an organization does to profitably meet customer needs. Treating marketing as a function dooms an organization.

Second, an effective planning process must be focused on the recommendations: the objectives, strategic initiatives, and tactics. A process that leads to people spending time on analysis at the expense of the recommendations is simply counterproductive. The focus has to be on the output and the implications.

Third, the planning process must ultimately produce decisions. The reason to write a marketing plan is to set the direction for the business. Setting the direction is all about making decisions. A good planning process, then, will lead to decisions. The process has a defined end point, when the team gets the green light and can move ahead with execution.

Fourth, a marketing planning process needs an owner and champion. A process without a clear owner will not take root; someone needs to drive the process, set the dates, and clarify the deliverables. Without a clear champion, a marketing plan process will not take hold.

Finally, the planning process needs senior management support. Ultimately, the priorities of an organization are driven from the top. As a result, the best marketing plan processes are supported by the CEO. The CEO doesn't have to review the marketing plan for every product; this is impractical and unrealistic. However, the CEO should be certain plans are being created, highlight the importance of the plans, and review the plans for key products and divisions.

Importantly, speed is not a characteristic of great marketing plans, for the simple reason that developing a great plan takes time. A plan that is assembled in a hurry often ends up being a copy of the prior year's plan; it adds no value. It is far better to take the time and effort required to do a good job. As Malcolm McDonald wrote in his book *Marketing Plans*. "Producing an effective marketing plan that will give your organization competitive advantage is not easy. It takes knowledge, skills, intellect, creativity, and, above all, time."[3]

One marketer described how his company rolled out new planning process, where every business unit was asked to finish the entire process in a matter of weeks. As you might expect, the new process failed—there wasn't enough time to flesh out the strategy. This particular marketer describes the situation, saying, "There wasn't enough time for critical thinking. It became 'we have to fill out the template.' It ended up being an unbridled mess."

A marketing plan process should take the time required to address the issues facing the business and present a credible plan for the future.

How Much Should a Marketing Plan Change from Year to Year?

Strategic initiatives and tactics should evolve over time; it would be odd indeed if tactics on a business were the same every year. The positioning of a business should be consistent, but the initiatives should change. Indeed, if you find that the initiatives in a plan are not changing, it is important to ask why.

One day in early September 2000, I decided to clean out the files in my office. At the time I was a senior category business director at Kraft Foods, responsible for running a collection of brands with annual sales of more than $500 million. I had recently moved into the role, and in the process I moved into my predecessor's office.

So I set aside some time and started opening up the cabinets. They were full of papers and reports and documents. And about a decade's worth of marketing plans.

I cracked open the marketing plan for 1993, an enormous document that described a challenging business situation and identified issues that had to be addressed. I then opened the marketing plan for 1994. Although the pages were different, the theme was the same; the plan described the same challenging business situation and identified the same issues that had to be addressed. I then opened the plan from 1995 and read about the same thing. It went on and on. The marketing plans were all different but all essentially the same. The situation hadn't changed substantially.

Each marketing plan, however, was long and detailed and thorough. It was clear that a talented team of people had spent weeks and weeks creating the plans.

Unfortunately, nothing happened and nothing changed; the same plan could have been presented in any year. The entire exercise was a waste of time.

A marketing plan should be a living document, changing to reflect the situation facing a business. A static marketing plan indicates a lack of creativity (no new ideas) or a lack of effectiveness (no progress), or both.

How is a Marketing Plan Different from a Business Plan?

Marketing plans are similar to business plans; both documents set the course for a business and highlight how the business will deliver sales and profits over time.

However, the two documents are different because business plans generally include many more topics, including operations strategy, financing issues, and human resource issues. Marketing is one just topic within a business plan.

To an extent, a good marketing plan provides the driving theme for a business plan. The marketing plan provides the spark and the big picture. The business plan includes all the functional activities that need to occur to keep the entire organization moving ahead.

Isn't a Long Marketing Plan a Sign of a Savvy Marketer?

Smart marketers do not create long marketing plans. Indeed, the reverse is true; people who are gifted at marketing produce tight, focused, compelling marketing plans.

To an extent, the size of a marketing plan reflects the level of marketing savvy of an organization. A company that doesn't understand and value marketing might not have a marketing plan at all. If there is a formal plan, it will probably be very superficial, because nobody spends much time on it and nobody cares about it very much.

As a company becomes more marketing focused, marketing plans tend to get longer and more thorough; the business team uncovers more information and data and includes that information in the plan. Indeed, some of the longest and most ineffective marketing plans are created by organizations that realize marketing is important, but have yet to understand and apply the insight that knowing things about your customer doesn't lead to better results; you have to actually do something with the learning.

Companies that are extremely savvy often have very tight, refined marketing plans; the organization understands that focus is essential and that what matters isn't how much people know, it is what they actually do. P&G, for example, is one of the leading marketing companies in the world. Marketing teams at P&G routinely produce very short, focused marketing plans with about six pages. Steven Cunliffe, president of Nestlé's frozen foods division, presents marketing plans for his billion-dollar organization in 20 pages.

Do I Really Have to Know This Stuff?

The honest answer is that no, you don't have to know how to write a great marketing plan. You don't have to pass an exam to write a marketing plan. The local police won't be after you if you keep writing long, traditional, and ineffective plans. The American Marketing Association doesn't issue citations for poor plans. Indeed, in some organizations you will be very safe sticking with the usual approach.

However, there are very few things you can do to help your career more than learning how to create a great marketing plan. This is true for several reasons.

First, great marketing plans are very often approved. As a result, creating a good marketing plan means you will have the opportunity to actually implement your ideas. Since results ultimately matter most, having the opportunity to implement your ideas is essential. Coming up with great ideas that never get implemented is both frustrating and dangerous; you have to actually do something to have an impact.

Second, in most organizations, marketing plans are very visible. Marketing plans are generally reviewed by very senior executives. As a result, marketers who develop tight, focused, and compelling plans simply look smarter and more capable than executives who develop weak plans. As every marketing executive knows perceptions matter most, being known as a smart, savvy leader is a very good thing.

David Hirschler has spent years leading brands at Colgate and Liz Claiborne. He observed that the people who create strong marketing plans stand out in an organization. According to Hirschler, "If you're really good at it, it's going to say good things about you." Similarly, executives who develop confused plans that lack focus inevitably look bad. Hirschler continued, "You can be a great marketer, but if you have a muddled presentation you aren't going to be well regarded."

Third, marketing plans can be time consuming, so executives who are efficient at writing them get more done. People who struggle writing plans end up having to devote far more time to the task. Being able to construct a strong plan in a relatively short period of time is a competitive advantage among peers at a similar level.

It is very difficult for a tennis player to win a match if he can't serve well. The serve in tennis is an essential, core skill; it starts the game. A good serve doesn't guarantee that a player will win the match, but a terrible serve virtually guarantees a loss.

Similarly, it is very difficult for a marketer to be successful if she can't create a good marketing plan. Creating powerful marketing plans is a core skill. The ability to create a good plan doesn't guarantee success, but a bad plan, or no plan, virtually guarantees less than optimal results.

Isn't This All Pretty Obvious?

It is indeed. The core ideas presented in this book are not revolutionary: create a plan, be clear on your objectives, focus on a few important strategic initiatives, and provide compelling support for your recommendation. As marketer Greg Wozniak noted, "It's almost scary how basic it is. It sounds almost too basic."

Simple or not, the reality is that many, many companies create marketing plans that are a disaster; they are too long, too complicated, too focused on random facts. The plan and the big ideas are obscured by the weight of the data and somewhat irrelevant pieces of information.

Sergio Pereira of Conagra summarized the situation well, explaining, "So much of marketing is common sense, but it all goes away when you write marketing plans."

Source Notes

This book is based on both research and personal experience.

Over the past four years, I have talked to dozens of marketing executives about how to create a good marketing plan. I talked to people running businesses, people who have written and reviewed marketing plans. It only makes sense to build a book about marketing plans based on input from practicing executives, because these are the people with the most experience in the field. Academic theory is relevant for marketing plans, of course, but a marketing plan is a tool, and the people with the keenest sense for how to create a better tool are the people who use the tool all the time.

The executives I met with worked at a wide range of organizations, including large, well-established companies and start-ups. I met with executives from industries including consumer packaged goods, health care, financial services, industrial chemicals, and technology. Many of the people I spoke with had global experience. Most of the people I interviewed were marketers by training, though almost all of them considered themselves general managers. Indeed, a good marketer is really a business leader. In my research I spoke with executives who had experience at many of the world's leading companies, including Nestlé, Unilever, Johnson & Johnson, Eli Lilly, Kodak, Pepsi, Prudential, and Pfizer. In total, the executives I interviewed had written or reviewed more than 1,000 marketing plans.

This book also draws on my own experiences creating and using marketing plans. Before joining the faculty at Northwestern University's Kellogg School of Management, I spent 11 years in marketing at Kraft Foods. At Kraft, each summer was marked by the annual marketing plan process. I wrote and reviewed dozens of marketing plans at Kraft for brands including Miracle Whip, Taco Bell, DiGiorno, A.1. steak sauce, Parkay margarine, Seven Seas salad dressing, and Bulls-Eye BBQ sauce. In addition, I headed up the marketing planning process for key business units. During my time at Kraft, I wrote a few wonderful marketing plans, and I wrote a few clunkers. I learned from both. Since joining the Kellogg faculty, I have had the opportunity to work directly with many of the world's best companies, such as Microsoft, Ford, Sony, JPMorganChase, General Electric, and BP.

Finally, this book reflects my experiences at Kellogg, where I have taught some of the best and brightest marketing students in the world. For almost a decade, I have taught a course on marketing strategy. As part of the class, students participate in a business simulation in which they manage a company over the course of seven periods. Each period, the students create plans and implement programs; they can launch new products, change prices, invest in advertising, expand and reduce their sales force. During the simulation, I have students write and present marketing plans. This has been an eye-opening experience for me. After reviewing more than 1,000 of these marketing plans, I have learned that some things work and some things don't. Most importantly, I have seen firsthand that people don't naturally write great marketing plans; it is a skill that has to be learned through instruction and experience.

1 WHO NEEDS A MARKETING PLAN, ANYWAY?

1. "Marketing 50," *Advertising Age* (November 12, 2007), p. S1.
2. Malcolm McDonald, *Marketing Plans*, 5th edition (Oxford: Butterworth-Heinemann), p. 13.
3. Michael E. Porter, Jay W. Lorsch, and Nitin Nohria, "Seven Surprises for New CEOs," *Harvard Business Review* (October, 2004), p. 71.
4. Noel Tichy and Ram Charan, "Speed, Simplicity, Self-Confidence: An Interview with Jack Welch," *Harvard Business Review* (September–October, 1989), p. 3.
5. Lynn Lunsford, "New Company, Same Problems for Ford's CEO," *Wall Street Journal* (September 7, 2006), p. B10.

2 WHY SO MANY MARKETING PLANS ARE A WASTE OF TIME

1. Mercedes M. Cardona, "CMOs under Fire," *Advertising Age* (May 3, 2004), p. 81.
2. Malcolm McDonald, *Marketing Plans*, 5th edition (Oxford: Butterworth-Heinemann), p. 31.
3. Rajat Gupta and Jim Wendler, "Leading Change: An Interview with the CEO of P&G," *McKinsey Quarterly, Web Exclusive* (July 29, 2005).
4. Noel Tichy and Ram Charan, "Speed, Simplicity, Self-Confidence: An Interview with Jack Welch," *Harvard Business Review* (September–October, 1989), p. 3.
5. William M. Luther, *The Marketing Plan*, 3rd edition (New York: AMACOM, 2001), p. xiii.
6. McDonald, p. 286.

3 WHAT REALLY MATTERS: THE ONE-PAGE SUMMARY

1. Development Dimensions International Inc.'s 2005 survey of 4,559 corporate managers in 36 countries, as cited in "All Talk?" *Business Week* (March 6, 2006), p. 13.
2. Thomas A. Stewart and Louise O'Brien, "Execution without Excuses," *Harvard Business Review* (March, 2005), p. 106.

3. Ilan Brat and Bryan Grulet, "Global Trade Galvanizes Caterpillar," *Wall Street Journal* (February 26, 2007), p. B7.

4. Paul Davies and Joann S. Lublin, "As Crises Pile Up, Bristol CEO Relies on Board Allies," *Wall Street Journal* (July 1, 2005), p. 1.

5. Malcolm McDonald, *Marketing Plans*, 5th edition (Oxford: Butterworth-Heinemann), p. 49.

6. Eli Lilly and Company submission to the U.S. Food and Drug Administration, August 10, 2004, p. 15. Study can be viewed at: http://www.fda.gov/ohrms/dockets/dailys/04/aug04/082404/04d-0042-c00034-vol3.pdf (accessed on April 15, 2008).

4 THE BEST OF THE BEST

1. Thomas A. Stewart and Louise O'Brien, "Execution without Excuses," *Harvard Business Review* (March, 2005), p. 110.

2. "Top 10 Leadership Tips from Jeff Immelt," *Fast Company* (April, 2004), p. 96.

3. James M. Kilts, *Doing What Matters* (New York: Crown Business, 2007), p. 24.

4. Barry Schwartz, *The Paradox of Choice* (New York: HarperCollins, 2004), p. 23.

5. Daisy Wademan, "The Best Advice I Ever Got," *Harvard Business Review* (January, 2005), p. 44.

6. Noel Tichy and Ram Charan, "Speed, Simplicity, Self-Confidence: An Interview with Jack Welch," *Harvard Business Review* (September–October, 1989), p. 4.

7. Sheena S. Iyengar and Mark R. Lepper, "When Choice Is Demotivating: Can One Desire Too Much of a Good Thing?," *Journal of Personality and Social Psychology* (December, 2000).

5 THE ROAD MAP: STEP BY STEP

1. James C. Collins and Jerry I. Porras, "Building Your Company's Vision," *Harvard Business Review* (September–October, 1996), p. 65.

2. Thomas A. Stewart and Louise O'Brien, "Execution without Excuses," *Harvard Business Review* (March, 2005), p. 109.

3. Collins and Porras, p. 73.

4. John J. Gabarro and John P. Kotter, "Managing Your Boss," *Harvard Business Review* (January, 2005), p. 98.

5. Daisy Wademan, "The Best Advice I Ever Got," *Harvard Business Review* (January, 2005), p. 44.

6. Susan Carey, "Changing the Course of JetBlue," *Wall Street Journal* (June 21, 2007), p. B2.

7. Kortney Stringer and Ann Zimmerman, "Polishing Penny's Image," *Wall Street Journal* (May 7, 2004), p. B5.

6 WRITING THE PLAN

1. Peter F. Drucker, "Managing Oneself," *Harvard Business Review* (January, 2005), p. 103.

2. Thomas A. Stewart and Louise O'Brien, "Execution without Excuses," *Harvard Business Review* (March, 2005), p. 108.

3. Daisy Wademan, "The Best Advice I Ever Got," *Harvard Business Review* (January, 2005), p. 44.
4. Noel Tichy and Ram Charan, "Speed, Simplicity, Self-Confidence: An Interview with Jack Welch," *Harvard Business Review* (September–October, 1989), p. 3.

7   THE BIG SHOW

1. Bob Garfield, *And Now a Few Words from Me* (New York: McGraw-Hill, 2003), p. 138.
2. Herminia Ibarra and Kent Lineback, "What's Your Story?" *Harvard Business Review* (January, 2005), p. 71.
3. Daniel Okrent, "Numbed by the Numbers, When They Just Don't Add Up," *New York Times* (January 23, 2005), section 4, p. 2.
4. Remarks of Bill Gates at Harvard University Commencement, June 7, 2007. Full text is at: http://www.news.harvard.edu/gazette/2007/06.14/99-gates. html (accessed on April 15, 2008).

11   COMMON QUESTIONS

1. Julie Schlosser, "Don't Picture the Audience Naked," *Fortune* (November 25, 2002), p. 46.
2. John A. Byrne, "The Fast Company Interview: Jeff Immelt," *Fast Company* (July, 2005), p. 64.
3. Malcolm McDonald, *Marketing Plans*, 5th edition (Oxford: Butterworth-Heinemann), p. xvii.

ACKNOWLEDGMENTS

One of the great things about working in the world of marketing is that you have the opportunity to collaborate with smart, dynamic people. It is not a solitary pursuit.

Dozens of people contributed to this book in different ways. My only concern is that it is impossible to note everyone who helped with the project.

The marketing executives I interviewed for this work, many of whom are named and quoted in the text, shared insights and best practices. In many ways, they are the heart of the book. I am much in their debt. In particular, Roland Jacobs and Stuart Baum read early drafts and provided constructive feedback. Greg Wozniak shared his insights and helped refine my thinking in several critical areas. Mark Silveira, author of *Ordinary Advertising. And How to Avoid It Like the Plague* encouraged me to keep the project moving and provided invaluable advice on the writing process. The Marketing Executives Networking Group (MENG) helped me connect with many sharp and savvy marketers and provided a valuable forum for sharing ideas. I am lucky to be part of the group.

I am grateful to the leadership team at Flahavan's, John Flahavan and John Noonan, for allowing me to use their company as the marketing plan example included in the book.

I am particularly in debt to my students at Northwestern University's Kellogg School of Management. For almost decade they have challenged me, kept me on my toes, and pushed me to refine and tighten my thinking and frameworks.

The marketing faculty at the Kellogg School of Management helped enormously with this project, providing both inspiration and good ideas. Greg Carpenter, Lakshman Krishnamurthi, Phil Kotler, Julie Hennessy, and Alex Chernev all made substantial contributions to the book. I had the very good fortune to work with Alice Tybout on *Kellogg on Branding*. That project convinced me to actually undertake this book. Andrew Razeghi, Steven Rogers, and Bob Schieffer, all recent authors, deserve particular note for having encouraged me to pursue the project and sharing insights from their experience. My administrator, Subarna Ranjit, helped me with this project from the very start. I am also in debt to Dean Dipak Jain for his support and leadership.

My agent, David Hale Smith, provided useful guidance and helped make this book a reality. The team at Palgrave Macmillan, including Airie Stuart,

Laurie Harting, and Emma Hamilton, has been supportive and encouraging from day one.

I am particularly thankful to editor Patty Dowd Schmitz, who worked closely with me on this book. Her candid feedback was both motivating and helpful. The imperfections in the book are purely my responsibility; Patty did all she could.

Finally, I am in debt to my family, Carol, Claire, Charlie, and Anna, for making me laugh and reminding me that the key to good life, like the key to a good marketing plan, is focusing on the things that matter most.

Index